GLIMPSES OF MUGHAL SOCIETY AND CULTURE

GLIMPSES OF MUGHAL SOCIETY AND CULTURE

– A Study Based on Urdu Literature: in the 2nd Half of the 18th Century

ISHRAT HAQUE

CONCEPT PUBLISHING COMPANY, NEW DELHI-110059

ISBN 81-7022-382-2

First Published 1992

Published and Printed by
Ashok Kumar Mittal
Concept Publishing Company
A/15-16, Commercial Block, Mohan Garden
NEW DELHI 110059 (India)

Lasertypeset by
Microtech Advance Printing Systems (Pvt.) Ltd.
H-13, Bali Nagar
NEW DELHI 110015

To my mother
and father

FOREWORD

Dr. Ishrat Haque has blazed a trail by treading a treacherous path which others fear to enter. Instead of commonality of ground between history and literature as both deal with the ebb and flow of 'social formation' in all its variegated hues, one is based on facts and the other thrives on imagination. The polarisation is perennial and looked from this angle, even the poetry at best is 'fiction' — a non-fact. Whatever, reality literature may claim to 'reflect' or 'portray', in fact as the nature of literature goes, it is the 'reconstruction' of reality, or the 'illusion' of reality, whose main objective is the 'aesthetic effect' as compared to the 'knowledge effect' which is the goal of history (both terms as developed and used by the neo-marxist French Philosopher Louis Althusser in *For Marx*, Harmonds Worth, Allen Lane, 1969). We may however, qualify the 'knowledge effect' by adding 'of perfective, of what has happened, or what has passed'.

Nonetheless, be it the reflection, or the illusion or a mere form, the poetical image springs from the hard 'social formation', which if studied and analysed with proper care and sensibility, may yield such information which cannot be culled from any other source. It is this rare treatment which Dr. Ishrat Haque has successfully applied to the late eighteenth century Urdu poetry. She has not restricted her study to the descriptive genres of *Shahr-ashob* and the *Qasida*, which given to hyperbole, bubble with surface information, but she has delved deep into the oblique and highly dense genre of the *Ghazal* which reverberates with the tragic undertones of the crumbling Mughal Empire tinged with the glow of its golden twilight. It is here that her study attains its high illuminative not only for the historian, but also for the literati who views literature as a socio-political by-product. There is thus a lot of interest for the intrepid traveller who wants to look beyond the barrier of disciplines.

Professor of Urdu
University of Delhi
5th March, 1990

GOPI CHAND NARANG

PREFACE

In the present study an attempt has been made to examine the historical content in the Urdu poetry of the second half of the eighteenth century. The high quality of literature produced in India during this period, including Urdu poetry made a significant contribution to the intellectual and cultural developments of the period. It would therefore be futile to brand the great literary output of the age as a part of a 'decadent' age, rather it was symbolic of the cultural and artistic achievements of the eighteenth century (Chapter 1). A word of caution however needs to be added. In any evaluation of the poetry a distinction must be made between the objective reflection of social reality in their poetry and the poets' own understanding of this reality. Also, due consideration has to be given to the great exaggeration and hyperbole which was the poet's right in the eighteenth century.

With the exception of Nazir Akbarabadi, all the poets under study, namely, Mir Taqi Mir, Mirza Rafi Sauda, Shah Hatim and Mir Dard spent the greater part of their lives in Delhi (Chapter 2) and were a witness to the last days of Mughal splendour in the reign of Muhammad Shah when the capital was a model of luxury and culture for the rest of India. They also saw this society suffer a severe set back in the years 1739-1760 which left a deep imprint on their writings. The passing away of the old order in Delhi, therefore, forms a constant theme of lament in their poetry. Although aware of the rise of the British power and its success in Bengal, the world of Mir and Sauda remained steeped in Mughal times. Such an attitude of the poets could be due to the fact that the great centres of Urdu poetry, especially Delhi and Agra still lay outside the influence of the British. Not surprisingly, therefore, the socio-political theme of their poetry centred around Delhi and its environs. The present work ends with the British occupation of Delhi in 1803 when the Mughal emperor Shah Alam II came under the protection of the East India Company.

The decline of the Mughal empire notwithstanding the idea of imperial authority, also voiced by poets like Mir and Sauda, remained embodied in the Mughal dynastic rule while every aspirant for political power including the British continued to seek legitimacy in the name of the Mughal emperor through out the eighteenth century. The poets who saw the decline of the nobles with the initial sense of shock and dismay reconciled to the political realities by pinning their faith and hope in the establishment or law and order by a section of the nobles at provincial or local levels (Chapter 4). The period thus witnessed a realignment of political power leading to the emergence of regional and local centres of political and economic activity as well as patronage of art and literature.

It is not possible to examine all the aspects of society on the basis of the writings of the poets. The chief purpose of the study is to analyse the attitudes and relationships, the value system and the socio-religious outlook which finds natural expression in literature (Chapter 6) rather than a detailed account of material conditions under such conventional heads as food, drink, clothes, means of recreation etc. The writings of the poets, especially in case of sufi poets like Mir Dard reveal at least at some levels of society a broader outlook in socio-religious matters and a steady growth of the forces of liberalism and eclecticism (Chapter 5) which find free expression in the Urdu ghazal of the age.

A word on the references and foot notes seems necessary here. Instead of following the common pattern of putting the surname of the author later, I have written, in case of the poets, the surname first, because the poets under study were known mostly by their surnames e.g. Mirza Mohammad Rafi Sauda as Sauda and Mir Taqi Mir as Mir etc.

I wish to express my sincere thanks to Professor Satish Chandra without whose supervision and guidance the work could not have been undertaken. I am especially grateful to Professor Nural Hasan for his valuable suggestions and encouragement. I am grateful to Professor Gopi Chand Narang, Professor S.R. Kidwai, Prof. H.C. Verma, and Dr. Muzaffar Alam for their comments and help in the translation and interpretation of many verses. My special thanks are due to my colleagues, Ms. Shashikala Mutatkar and Ms. Vidyabati Das Arora, who gave many fruitful suggestions in improving this work. Finally I am deeply indebted to my father Mirza Iqbal Shah, whose constant help has been a continuous source of encouragement in the writing of this work.

ISHRAT HAQUE

CONTENTS

1

THE EIGHTEENTH CENTURY BACKGROUND

The Age is not like the previous one Mir
The times have changed, the earth and sky have changed.[1]

اس عہد کو نہ جانے اگلا سا عہد میرؔ ؎ وہ دور اب نہیں وہ زمیں آسماں نہیں

By mid-eighteenth century the empire of the Mughals which had spread to twenty two subahs in the reign of Aurangzeb lay confined to Delhi and its immediate neighbourhood. The gloomy political situation highlighted by this decline, however, did not necessarily imply the collapse of the political system established by the Mughals or an all round decay and stagnation of society.[2] The dismissal of the eighteenth century as an era of darkness can be explained partly in terms of the utilization of such restricted source material as the court chronicles which recorded the decline of Mughal dynastic rule or the accounts of foreign travellers and missionaries in the late eighteenth and early nineteenth centuries which spoke of large scale desolation in North India while highlighting the 'ignorance', illiteracy and semi-barbarism the authors claimed to have seen around themselves. The judgement pronounced proclaimed the age as one of all round decay and stagnation, political, intellectual and moral. This cultural decline was emphasized, along with political weakness to explain the success of the British in India in the nineteenth century.[3] It is not historically correct to assume a general decadence of the state and particularly of the society exclusively in terms of the decline of the imperial power. Medieval social organizations and institutions in fact showed great vitality in survival and remarkable continuity and adaptability especially at the village and qasbah levels, to rapid political change during the eighteenth century.[4] Mughal revenue administration survived not only in the independent 'subahs' but several newly founded kingdoms adopted the Mughal system with regional variations.[5]

Politically, the destruction of the empire did not bring to an end the idea of imperial government as embodied in the Mughal theory of sovereignty. It survived even during the years 1759-1770 when the emperor, Shah Alam II (1759-1806), lived in exile in Allahabad and the capital remained without its imperial head, no attempt was made by any power to seize the throne and end the Mughal dynastic rule. As none of the contending powers possessed the necessary resources or moral sanction of the people to replace the Mughals, the Marathas, Afghans and the British continued to seize power and exercise it in the name of the Mughal emperors. It is even argued that the nature of the seizure of power and adoption of Mughal Political and administrative systems did not essentially lead to the final dissolution of the empire but may be said to have initiated new cycles of growth.[6]

The idea of Delhi as the seat of the imperial government remained popular even with the Marathas and the East India Company which emerged as the two Chief contending powers for the control of the emperor and the Delhi government in the last quarter of the century. The Marathas had encouraged the Mughal emperor in exile to seek their protection in order to facilitate his return to his ancestral seat of power in 1771. The British too realized the importance of the imperial name and for a long time tried to neutralize the influence of the Marathas over Delhi court and made elaborate arrangements to receive Prince Mirza Jawan Bakht, heir apparent, who had fled from the capital and taken shelter in Benaras in 1784.[7] In 18th century India it was a normal practice to grant shelter and pension to fleeing Mughal princes. Shah Alam himself had been given protection by the Nawabs of Awadh and later the East India Company before he returned to Delhi. As late as 1789 a Mughal Prince, Mirza Ali Bakht Bahadur Muhammad Zahiruddin Azfari escaped from the palace and wrote a diary of his travels which shows that through out his wanderings he was treated with respect and honour due to a Mughal prince. The rulers of Jaipur, Awadh and Carnatic considered it their honour to accord him such a treatment.[8] The Raja of Jaipur, Sawai Pratap Singh, presented a Nazar to the prince and even refused to sit in his presence.[9] The Delhi government as the nominal suzerain power also continued to receive imperial gifts (Nazars) even when the flow of revenues had entirely stopped in the late eighteenth century. Indeed as late as the middle of the nineteenth century when the Mughal rule barely extended beyond the red fort in Delhi, Bahadur Shah Zafar became the obvious rallying point for the rebels in 1857.

Political decay though evident at the court, political life in independently subahs revealed a different pattern altogether where political and economic affairs were conducted with vigour and efficiency till the beginning of British intervention. The traditional Mughal policy based on the principle of balancing various ethnic, regional and local elements was adopted to a large extent by the independent rulers of Bengal, Awadh, Hyderabad and other states. In Bengal realizing the weakness of the central government after the death of Aurangzeb, Murshid Quli Khan used his freedom to consolidate his position in Bengal by gaining the support and loyalty of nobles, Zamindars, and financial interests including the great banking house of Jagat Seths.[10] The second half of the eighteenth century witnessed the stabilization of the Hyderabad State in the long reign of Nizam Ali Khan (1762-1803) who also shifted the capital from Aurangabad to Hyderabad. Although the first Nizam had been known for his Turani affiliations, he had been liberal enough to appoint many Hindus to high offices.[11] The old Hyderabad nobility of Mughal times gradually gave way to new elements which included large number of non-muslims, especially Marathas and Rajputs, who had earlier served the Deccan Sultanates. A large number of Hindu bankers, money-lenders and clerical castes like the Kayasthas of the north formed the new ruling class of the state. By late eighteenth century, among the ten leading noble families, only one was sunni, five were shias and four were Hindus.[12] The rulers of Awadh faced with the hostility of the old Mughal nobility utilized the power of local social groups to counter their opposition. Nawab Shujauddaulah, for instance, decided to rid himself of the old nobility which had served him so poorly at Buxar in 1764.[13] He recruited a large number of Shaikhzadas, Telingana Rajputs and Gosain mercenaries, the so-called 'low born' elements, to strengthen the military power of the state.[14]

The independent states of the eighteenth century thus continued the Mughal methods of political manipulation and liberal attitude in matters of recruitment and towards cultural syncretism. The state of Awadh freely enlisted Hindus to position of military and administrative importance, patronizing non-Muslims and non-shias alike.[15] Similar attitude was adopted by the Nawabs of Bengal[16] while in Hyderabad state, Hindus and Shias dominated the administration.[17] The same trend may be noted in other parts of India including Maratha and Sikh territories. The effort to follow the pattern set by the Mughals perhaps became more intense in the eighteenth century as regional powers were seeking legitimisation of their own authority as political heir to the Mughal heritage.

The Islamic concept of state preached by orthodox leaders was largely ignored by the Muslim rulers of the period. Contrary to the claims of Muslim religious leaders and theologians like Shah Waliullah political groupings and conflicts during the eighteenth century were motivated by expediency cutting across religious and sectarian considerations. Even in 1761, an alliance of Muslim powers such as Nizamulmulk Najibuddaulah and Ahmad Shah Abdali to eradicate 'Hindu' dominance[18] remained a futile dream of Shah Waliullah. Both the Nizam and Najibuddaulah were primarily concerned with the extension of their local power rather than in uniting Muslims against the Hindu opponents of the empire. The escape of Malhar Rao after the defeat at Panipat, for instance, was managed by Najibuddaulah in return for services earlier rendered to him in Delhi by the Maratha leader against Imadulmulk.[19] As for Ahmad Shah, although he was chiefly concerned with the defeat of the Marathas and the protection of his provinces in the Punjab, restoration of Muslim power, protection of sunnis or annihilation of polytheism were purely secondary issues.

The establishment of political stability in many independent subahs resulted in corresponding economic growth and prosperity in different parts of India. The rulers sought to establish greater control on the resources of agriculture and landed elements like Zamindars, intermediaries and the peasants. The method of revenue farming, considered an evil practice during the Mughal times, became a common practice in the days of the later Mughals[20] as it was found impossible to revitalize the system of direct collection. Continuous warfare left an adverse impact on agricultural production and the movement of armies destroyed wells and irrigation tanks leading to the migration of peasants to areas of peace and security. The migration of peasants, however, helped in opening up old fallow and virgin lands for cultivation. The rulers of Rohilkhand and Awadh encouraged the growth of new crops including planting of fruits such as mango, guava and other fruit trees around their states. These gardens brought considerable income to land-holders and played a significant role in local economies.[21] Many independent states encouraged agriculture through revenue remissions (taqavi) and low revenue rates on newly opened land while duties on merchandize were lowered and even abolished.[22] Even the Rohillas generally condemned by contemporary

British writers are praised by Forster writing in 1780s for being among the few Muslim rulers in India who played a direct role in stimulating the agricultural prosperity of their region.[23]

Political instability and armed conflict notwithstanding, evidence of economic stability and growth are evident in many parts of the country during the eighteenth century. While views differ on the nature, extent and possibilities of capitalistic development[24] in the last decades of the century, it is suggested that the problem should be examined at regional levels rather than on an all India basis.[25] Economic groups such as traders and bankers were certainly gaining in power, a development noted by contemporary European writers but their power differed from region to region. Thus, from the "enormously wealthy bankers of Maratha territories absolutely rolling in wealth", who were occupied in the "exclusive pursuit of sordid and selfish gains"[26] to the great bankers of Bengal, the power and influence of these groups had certainly increased in the eighteenth century. War and political upheaval thus did not always destroy trade and production and merchants and bankers strengthened their hold on the working of the revenue system by financing the deficits of the Rajas and clan leaders and also working on taqavi loans given to the cultivators in the villages.[27] The power of the Hindu commercial groups also increased in the kingdoms of Awadh, Rohilkhand and Bengal. Although the merchants and commercial groups had considerably increased their power and influence, the military aristocracies dominated the political and cultural life making it virtually impossible for merchants to aspire for direct political power in the eighteenth century.

Political decentralization and military activity adversely affected the fate of the old imperial cities of Delhi, Agra and Lahore.[28] But several new cities east of Delhi[29] including Lucknow, Farrukhabad and Pilibhit emerged as flourishing centres of political, commercial and cultural life during the second half of the eighteenth century. As regards Delhi which forms the focus of this study, two significant factors need to be noticed. First, in the decline of Delhi, political factors such as the weakness of Mughal monarchy and the intense factionalism among the leading nobles for the appropriation of revenues, the pillaging activity by invading Jat, Maratha and Afghan forces were reinforced by ecological and climatic features.[30] These included the breakdown of the canal system in the mid-century that took away as many as 500 miles of territory out of cultivation. The deforestation of the Agra-Delhi region[31] and the great famine of 1782-1783 was far more destructive than all the wars put together.[32] Second, despite a prolonged period of devastation (1739-1760) economic activity in Delhi did not cease altogether.[33] The invaders like Nadir Shah and Ahmad Shah Abdali removed the hoarded treasures. There was, however, no long term impact on prices and on commerce and did not lead to a sharp downward trend in the Indian economy in the period immediately following the invasion.

Delhi recovered some stability and order during the strong regency of Najibuddaulah (1761-1770). The return of emperor Shah Alam II to the capital in 1772 and the rule of his all powerful minister and regent Mirza Najaf Khan[34] till the latter's death in 1782 provided the capital the much needed security and peace conducive to the growth of economic activity. Although Delhi from 1782-1784 again seemed to have plunged into an "anarchy",[35] following the death of Najaf Khan as the leading Mughal nobles fought among themselves for the position of the regent, economic and social life was not disrupted. Delhi in the years of Maratha occupation from 1784 onwards to the surrender of Shah Alam II to the British in 1803 remained a flourishing city despite the growing economic hardships of the emperor and his household and the bankruptcy of the regent Mahadaji Sindhia.[36] The capital suffered a shock during the outrage committed by Ghulam Qadir Rohilla on Shah Alam but his short occupation of the city (18th July to 2nd October, 1788) and subsequent lootings were confined to the palace, the members of the imperial family and the leading nobles while the trading communities and ordinary citizens did not suffer from extortion. The acute shortage of grain in the capital[37] during the period was temporary and normalcy was restored with the suppression of Ghulam Qadir and the restoration of Shah Alam in 1789.

In spite of having lost its primacy as a market of goods and services, the capital's trade and commerce were not totally disrupted during the second half of the eighteenth century. Delhi's long distance trade on old imperial routes continued though at a much reduced scale including trade links with Kashmir, Kabul and Central Asia.[38] Even as late as 1793 the once a year visiting caravans from the north brought Kabul horses, Kashmiri shawls and fruits. The last two commodities could be bought in Delhi at reasonable prices.[39] Though the bazaars, seemed to be 'indifferently furnished' and 'population reduced', cotton cloth was 'still manufactured' and corn rice, millet and indigo cultivated on the banks of the Jamuna.[40] Agra like Delhi though suffering from periodic set-backs due to military activity and lootings survived the vicissitudes of times, largely because of the economic stability provided by a ten mile agricultural belt surrounding the city.[41] Trade also continued, although at a reduced level, only insurance rates and charges were adjusted to take account of unfavourable political and climatic conditions.[42] Economic activity continued to be conducted with great vigour during the Maratha control of the city (1782-1803).

Society and State in the middle of the eighteenth century survived the onslaught of internecine warfare and rapid political change. The age did not also prove to be detrimental to the development of art, architecture, music, painting and poetry, at the capital as well as at the provincial levels. Delhi during the reign of Mohammad Shah, in spite of the idle levity and frivolity that characterized court life was inhabited by a large number of prominent writers, scholars, theologians, mystics and poets of all shades who richly contributed to the artistic and intellectual activity in the capital.[43] In spite of the essentially medieval milieu and the drawbacks of the traditional educational system along with the prevailing political instability, the period proved to be a most fertile one in terms of literary growth in different parts of India. Delhi which suffered from constant threat of invasion and political upheaval produced an amazing amount of literature consisting of mystical and theological writings as well as poetry, richly contributing to the cultural achievements of the period. The capital once the centre of Persian culture was now emerging as the centre of the growth of Urdu poetry which heralded a new era in Indo-Muslim cultural traditions.

The new literary medium in the form of Urdu which developed in the north, called Hindawi[44] up to the sixteenth century, may be seen in the context of rapid growth and development of regional literatures, in the declining years of the Mughal empire. These included literature in Sindhi, Punjabi, Bengali and Oriya.[45] As regards Urdu it had found its way to the Deccan in the late thirteenth and early years of the fourteenth century although it is not clear how this language was transferred to this region.[46] It could have been transported to the Deccan with the constant flow of Muslims, especially sufis who went to Deccan via Gujarat and Malwa from the thirteenth century onwards. The sufis played a significant role in the development of the language as they needed a medium that could be understood by the masses.[47] The Chishti saints of Bijapur including Shah Miranji (d. 1499) and his successors did not write exclusively in Persian but established Dakhani language as a recognized medium of sufi literature. It received its first recognition from the sultans of Golconda and Bijapur[48] and continued to flourish in the Deccan for more than a hundred and fifty years.

Urdu poetry gained great popularity in Delhi in the first quarter of the eighteenth century, a time when Urdu speaking people struggled to overcome the tyranny of Persian and began writing in their own vernacular. Such a process was greatly aided by the fact that most poets, with the exception of perhaps Sauda, came from professional, intellectual and sufi groups rather than aristocratic circles associated with Persian culture.[49] The visit of Wali (1667-1744) the leading poet of the Deccan to Delhi around 1700 is generally considered the beginning of the rise of Urdu poetry in Delhi. Wali met the leading poets of the city including the famous Naqshbandi saint, Shah Gulshan who also helped in popularizing Wali's poetry in Delhi. Wali himself expressed his admiration for the city and its people in the following couplet:

Will some one go and tell Muhammad Shah
Delhi has captured the heart of Wali.[50]

دل ولی کا لے لیا دلی نے چھین جا کہو کوئی محمد شاہ سوں

Wali's poems received a warm welcome in Delhi in view of the growing unpopularity of the increasing formalism of the Persian ghazal. The rise and popularity of Urdu poetry in fact symbolized the fruition in Delhi of liberal cultural traditions that had been taking shape in the past two centuries of Mughal rule. The broadening of the cultural base[51] during the eighteenth century was a significant process greatly helped by the rise and popularity of Urdu poetry. Mir in his tazkirah (Wr. 1754) mentions 103 poets[52] while Mushafi who wrote his account a few years later gives the names of 278 poets[53] while the number of Persian poets given is only 119 in his tazkirah of Persian poets.[54] The popularity of Urdu poetry was not confined to the Muslim upper classes in spite of having a largely Muslim background but extended also to other sections of society including a large number of Hindu poets.[55] The growing number of Urdu poets as well as their patrons who varied from the nobles and court circles to men of learning and sufis were participants in the eclectic culture of the age which came to enjoy a far wider social base than had ever been possible in the past.

The poets under study, namely Shah Hatim (1699-1791), Mirza Rafi Sauda (1713-1781). Mir Taqi Mir (1722-1810), Mir Dard (1719-1785) and Nazir Akbarabadi (1735-1830) did not confine themselves to the writings of mere eulogies or tales of romance, *(Hijr* and *wisal)*. On the contrary their poetry gave ample voice to such dominant features of the age as mysticism, liberalism and humanism which continued to shape the intellectual currents of the society throughout the eighteenth century. All the poets, with the exception of Nazir, who left Delhi in his boyhood, spent the greater part of their lives in the capital and were witness to the last days of Mughal splendour in the reign of Muhammad Shah, a time when Delhi was a model of luxury and culture to the rest of India. This society is admired and described by Hatim in a long poem entitled '*Bazm-i-Ishrat*',[56] written two years before the invasion and devastation of Delhi at the hands of Nadir Shah. The poet praises the Emperor Muhammad Shah and the city of Shajahanabad in the following verses:

> I had a Sudden impulse to say something in praise of Delhi,
> Delhi is not a city but a rose Garden
> Even its desert is more pleasing than an orchard,
> Beautiful women are the bloom of its streets and markets.
> Shy coquettish beauties are found at every step
> While every place is adorned with greenery and lovely cypress trees.
> Any one living in Hindustan in this age is the Shahjahan of his times.[57]

یکایک شوق یں بول اٹھا جی ؎ کہ کہتے اوّلاً تعریفِ دہلی
نہیں ہے شہر دہلی ہے گلستاں ؎ چمن سے جس کا خوشتر ہے بیاباں
ہر اک کی چشمِ قاتل مست و خونخوار ؎ ہر اک کے ابرواں باڑھ یل تر دار
وہ بے شک وقت کا شاہِ جہاں ہے ؎ جو کوئی متوطنِ ہندوستاں ہے

Hatim's description of Delhi of the pre-1739 period well compares with Dargah Quli Khan's account of the society of Delhi marked by the spirit of revelry, debauchery and opulence.[58] Hatim, Sauda, Mir and others saw this flourishing city repeatedly invaded, pillaged and looted from 1739 to 1760 which to the poet's perception, seemed an 'eclipse of a civilization' nurtured during the Mughal age, at the hands of the foreign invaders and the semi-barbarous Jat and Maratha soldiers. In the words of Sauda:

> O Sauda look what havoc vicissitudes have played
> Where not long ago there was merriment,
> Nothing is left except tearful eyes.[59]

دیکھ سودا گردشِ افلاک سے کیا کیا ہوا ؎ دورِ ساغر تھا ابھی یا ہے ابھی چشمِ پُرآب

The desolation of Delhi for the poets was no ordinary phase of history but seemed the ruin of a most cherished society. Hatim who had composed verses praising Delhi of Muhammad Shah's times wrote verses lamenting the turn of fortunes in so short a period.

How can one be happy even for a moment in this age
That is devoid of all that brings happiness:
The cup bearer, festivity and peace of mind
The constant flow of tears from my eyes
In fact comes from my heart
A cupful of sorrows brimming over.[60]

کہو کس طرح کوئی ہو خوشی یہاں ایک دم ایسے دور میں
نہ وہ بزم ہے نہ وہ ساقی ہے نہ وہ شوق ہے نہ فراغ دل
وہ چشم سے لگ لگ پلک سے بہر مژہ سے ڈھلک ڈھلک
یہاں قطرہ قطرہ چھلک چھلک مرا بہہ چلا ہے ایاغِ دل

The poets in Delhi suffered extreme hardships and a sense of insecurity due to the decline of patronage in the years 1739-40 and again in 1757-1760 which came in the wake of incessant warfare and looting of the capital. The large scale emigration of nobles, scholars and poets from the capital during this period to the neighbouring towns of Farrukhabad, Lucknow and the Jat kingdom must be examined in the light of the magnitude of destruction of not so much of the city, its trade or industry, but of the nobles, the men of political and economic standing who had offered patronage to the literati. To the poets, not only the age but even the people and their behaviour seemed to have undergone a change. Old relationships and values seemed to be losing their meaning in the ruthless pursuit of personal gains. Mir Dard, the sufi poet, condemns this attitude in the following words:

Greatness is no longer the privilege of kings
Whosoever can lay hand on the cup becomes Jamshed.[61]

سلطنت پر نہیں ہے کچھ موقوف ؎ جس کے ہاتھ آوے جام سو جم ہے

In this process of changing fortunes, the people with skill and talent dependent on the patronage of the nobles of the city, were bound to suffer most, which forms a subject of great lament for Sauda:

> An artist gains no recognition today
> Woe to the heart that is keen on learning art.[62]

دیکھی نہ ہنرمند کی میں قدر جہاں میں ؎ اے وائے براں دل جو طلبگار ہنر ہے

Both Mir and Sauda conclude that the age no longer rewarded virtue or talent. In such times a poet can only expect a life of hardship for there is no one to patronize his talent.

> All the craftsmen are ruined and I am one of them.
> It is a great sin to know your art in times like these.[63]

صنّاع ہیں سب خوار ازاں جملہ ہوں میں بھی ہے عیب بڑا اس میں جسے کچھ ہُنر آوے

The poets of Delhi bewail the fate of the literati of the city in a period of extreme dislocation of life and desolation following the invasion and occupation of Delhi by Ahmad Shah Abdali in 1757. Sauda wrote his two long *Shahr Ashobs* in the same year in which he describes the ruin of the city and the decline of the nobles of Delhi. Carefully examined his *Shahr Ashobs* reveal that far from merely repeating the traditional style of the poem.[64] Sauda concentrates on the devastation of the city in the years 1756-1757, the decline of the old nobility and its failure to offer patronage to professional groups, men of learning and talent.[65] Sauda himself confronted with the problem left Delhi for Farrukhabad in 1757 while Mir left for the Jat kingdom around 1760. The latter in his autobiography, narrates the misery of a number of nobles including Raja Jugal Kishore who advised Mir to seek shelter, elsewhere.[66] Sauda never returned to Delhi but Mir did so in 1772 in the hope of the revival of patronage in the capital.

The situation reflected in the poetry of Mir, Sauda and others needs to be examined with care taking into account the poetic hyperbole as well as the particular phase of Delhi's history at the time of the composition of the poetry. The picture of desolation drawn in Saudas' *Shehr Ashobs* and Mir's poems pertains to the period 1756-1760. Both the poets left the capital soon after the devastation. The picture of decline drawn by them, therefore, need not be generalized to imply a period of continuous decline for Delhi or for regions near the capital. The fact that the poets were able to seek and find new patrons in cities like Farrukhabad and Lucknow is an indication of the flourishing new centres of patronage not very far from Delhi. The exodus from Delhi of a large number of people attached to the court and notables of the city, poets and scholars including the family of Ghulam Husain Tabatabai,[67] the author of *Siyarul Mutakherin*, to the states of Farrukhabad, Lucknow and Murshidabad was indicative of the attitude of these groups towards the empire. This implied the realization of the impossibility of the revival of the fortunes of the empire and their willingness to sell their talent to new patrons who were fast replacing the old Mughal nobility.

Delhi, though having lost much of its earlier splendour continued to be inhabited by nobles, traders, poets and sufis. Contemporary accounts pertaining to the 1770s speak of a well populated city with a number of localities of different social or professional groups.[68] Economic activity in the capital, as noticed earlier, did not cease altogether. Murtaza Husain referring to the last decades of the century writes that all kinds of goods were available in Delhi. The main bazaar of Chandni Chowk, in comparison to the days of Muhammad Shah, gave a deserted look but other markets in Shahjahanabad like Khari Baoli and bazaar Khanum were full of activity.[69] A large number of notables had left the city in the decades, 1770s and 1780s yet a sizable Mughal nobility survived in Delhi because of its political role as an imperial city. The Muslim religious groups including the leading sufi saints like Mazhar Jan-i-Janan and Mir Dard, fulfilling the spiritual needs of the society, remained in the capital. The poet Hatim, who had early in life, adopted the ideal of darveshi too did not move out of Delhi and lived there till his death in 1791. Mir who had left Delhi in 1760 returned to the city in 1772 and continued to live there in extreme poverty till his departure for Lucknow in 1782. It was a period of comparative peace, prosperity and stability in Delhi. Yet Mir's inability to find a suitable patron, to some extent, can be taken as an indication of the disappearance of the old nobility of the pre-1760 era who had extended patronage to men of talent. Hence Mir's bitterness against a society that no longer seemed to appreciate his art. The emperor Shah Alam II, himself reduced to strained circumstances used to send for Mir occasionally, so did a few other nobles,[70] but no great noble came forward to offer the kind of protection and patronage desired by the poet. Delhi in the 1780s and 1790s was not lacking in men of wealth, only wealth seems to have changed hands. The new powerful patrons of the period namely the Marathas and the rising Jain and Khatri trading communities, who engaged themselves in great construction activity in the city, building houses, temples, gardens and rest houses[71] had little appreciation for poetry or poetic talent as well as intellectual activity or social life associated with it. Hence Mir's frustration at the decline of the poetical gatherings on his return to Delhi in the 1770s:

> Time was when connoisseurs listened
> Applausing each verse and thought at symposiums.[72]

کیا قدر تھی سخن کی جب یاں بھی صحبتیں تھیں ؎ ہر بات جائزہ ہے ہر بیت پر صلے ہیں

The lingering Mughal nobility offered patronage at a drastically reduced level which could hardly attract the best talent of the age to Delhi. The departure of Syed Insha after a brief stay in Delhi in 1774 to the court of Awadh may be noted in this context.[73] The poetry of Sauda, Mir, Hatim and Dard not merely symbolized the decline of the old order in Delhi but also a society and culture in a state of transition. The latter aspect found its fullest expression in the poetry of Nazir Akbarabadi which portrayed a cultural environment largely free of court influences during the eighteenth century.

NOTES

1. Mir Taqi Mir, *Kulliyat-i-Mir*, Allahabad, 1971, Volume I, p. 351.
2. H. Goetz, *Crisis of Indian Civilization in the eighteenth and early nineteenth centuries*, Calcutta, 1938, pp. 5-8, speaks of political and moral decay but lays stress on the cultural and aesthetic achievements of the age; Satish Chandra, *Parties and Politics at the Mughal Court 1707-1740*, New Delhi, 2nd edition, 1972, p. 263; and 'writing of Social History of Medieval India, Trends and Prospects' in *Medieval India: Society, Jagirdari Crisis and the Village*, New Delhi, 1982, p. 90; George Bearce, 'Culture of the Eighteenth century India — A reappraisal' *Indian History Congress*, 1961; 'Intellectual and cultural, characteristics of India in a changing Era 1740-1800', *Journal of Asian Studies*, 1965; C.A.

Bayly, *Rulers, Townsmen and Bazaars, North Indian Society in the Age of British Expansion, 1770-1870*, Cambridge, 1983; Muzaffar Alam, *The Crisis of Empire in Mughal North India, Awadh and Punjab 1707-48*, New Delhi, 1986.

3. J.S. Mill, *The History of British India*, 5th edition, London, 1858, Volume 10; For a critical assessment of this attitude see, Humayun Kabir, *Britain and India*, Calcutta, 1960, p. 28; George Bearce, *British Attitudes towards India*, 1784-1858, London, 1961, pp. 71-75.

4. Satish Chandra, 'Some Aspects of the growth of money economy in India during the seventeenth century in *Medieval India*, pp. 162-163, and 'Some Aspects of the Indian village society in North India during the eighteenth century', *The Indian Historical Review*, Volume I, 1974, pp. 61-62; B.R. Grover, 'The concept of village community in North India during the Mughal Age and the Pre-British Era', Institute of Advanced study, Simla, 1966, and Presidential Address, Proceedings of *Indian History Congress*, 1976, pp. 143-178; Nurul Hasan, *Thoughts on Agrarian Relations in Mughal India*, New Delhi, 1973, pp. 25-27.

5. Indu Banga, *Agrarian System of the Sikhs: Late 18th and early 19th century*, New Delhi, 1978, pp. 87, 181-82.

6. P. Spear, *Twilight of the Mughals*, 2nd edition, New Delhi, 1969, p. 9; Satish Chandra, *Parties and Politics*, p. 1; J.C. Heestermann, 'Western Expansion, Indian Reaction: Mughal Empire and British Raj' in *The Inner Conflict of Tradition*, (ed.) J.C. Heesterman, Chicago, 1985, pp. 162, 173.

7. *Palmer to Hastings, 29 October 1789 Bin. Add. MS.*, quoted P. Spear, *Twilight of the Mughals*, p. 29.

8. Muhamad Zahiruddin Azfari, *Waqiat-i-Azfari*, Translation, A. Sattar, Madras, 1937.

9. *Ibid.*, p. 41.

10. N.K. Sinha, *Economic History of Bengal*, Calcutta, 1962, Volume II, pp. 119-122; Abdul Karim, *Murshid Quli Khan and his times*, Dacca, 1963, pp. 49-50, 90-92, 99-100; Philip B. Calkins, 'The formulation of a regionally oriented ruling group in Bengal 1700-1740' *Journal of Asian Studies*, Volume XXIX, No. 4, 1970, p. 804.

11. Yusuf Husain Khan, *Nizamulmulk Asaf Jah I, Founder of the Hyderabad State*, Manglore, 1936, pp. 291-292.

12. Karen Leonard, 'The Hyderabad Political System and its Participants', *Journal of Asian Studies*, XXX, No. 3, 1971, p. 581.

13. Mustajab Khan, *Gulistan-i-Rehmat*, Translation, C. Elliott, *The life of Hafizool Moolk*, London, 1831, p. 85.

14. Najmul Ghani, *Tarikh-i-Awadh*, Lucknow, 1919, Volume II, pp., 153, 157-158; Muhammad Faiz Bakhsh, *Tarikh-i-Farah* Bakhsh, Translation, William Hoey, *Memoirs of Delhi and Faizabad*, Allahabad, 1889, Volume II, pp. 7, 13, 34.

15. Najmul Ghani, *Tarikh-i-Awadh*, Volume II, p. 311; A.L. Srivastava, *Shujaud-daulah of Awadh*, 2nd edition, Agra, 1974, Volume II, pp. 296-97.

16. Abdul Karim, *Murshid Quli Khan and His Times*, pp. 248-250.

17. H.K. Sherwani, 'Deccan the region of co-existence and integration', in *Medieval India, A Miscellany*, Bombay 1977, Volume IV, pp. 147-148.

18. K.A. Nizami, (ed.), *Shahwaliullah Ke Siyasi Maktubat*, Aligarh, 1950, pp. 118-119, 142-147.

19. Mustajab Khan, *Gulistan-i-Rahmat*, p. 66.

20. W.H. Moreland, *From Akbar to Aurangzeb: A Study in Indian Economic History*, New Delhi, 1972, pp. 239-240, 249-250; Noman Ahmad Siddiqi, *Land Revenue Administration under the Mughals, 1700-1759*, Bombay, 1970, pp. 2-3, 38-39.

21. Irfan Habib, 'Potentialities of capitalistic development in the economy of Mughal India', *Journal of Economic History* XXIX, 1969, p. 21.

22. Dilbagh Singh, 'Ijara system in eastern Rajasthan 1750-1800' *Proceedings of the Rajasthan History*, Congress VI, 1973, pp. 60-69; *Gulistan-i-Rehmat*, pp.87, 117.

23. G. Forster, *A Journey from Bengal to England through the northern parts of India, Kashmir, Afghanistan and Persia*, London, 1798, Volume I, p. 137.

24. Irfan Habib, 'Potentialities of capitalistic Development', V.I. Pavlov, *Indian Capitalist Class: A Historical Perspective*, Delhi, 1964; A.I. Chicherov, *Indian Economic Development in the Sixteenth to Eighteenth Centuries*, Moscow, 1971.

25. Satish Chandra, *The Eighteenth Century in India: Its Economy and the Role of the Marathas, the Jats, the Sikhs and the Afghans*, Calcutta, 1986, pp. 35-36.

26. H.T. Prinsep, *The History of the Political and Military Transactions in India during the administration of Marquess of Hastings 1813-1823*, London, 1825, Volume II, p. 298.

27. Dilbagh Singh 'The Role of Mahajans in the rural economy in Eastern Rajasthan during the eighteenth century', *Social Scientist*, May, 1974, pp. 21-23; S. Nurul Hasan, K.N. Hasan, S.P. Gupta 'Patterns of Agricultural Production in the Territories of Amber 1650-1750' *Indian History Congress*, 1966, pp. 244-248.

28. H.K. Naqvi, *Urban Centres and Industries in Upper India 1556-1803*, Bombay, 1968, pp. 12-20.

29. Tapan Ray Chaudhury, 'The mid-eighteenth century Background' in Dharma Kumar, (ed.), *The Cambridge Economic History of India*, New Delhi, 1984, Volume II, p.8.

30. C.A. Bayly, 'Delhi and other cities of North India during the Twilight' in R.E. Frykenberg, (ed.), *Delhi Through the Ages*, New Delhi, 1986, p. 230.

31. Irfan Habib, *Agrarian System of Mughal India*, Bombay, 1963, pp. 56-57.

32. P. Spear, *Twilight of the Mughals*, p. 116.

33. Murtaza Hussain, Translation, W. Irvine, 'Ahmad Shah Abdali and the Indian Wazir Imadulmulk', *Indian Antiquary*, XXVI, 1907, p. 60.

34. W. Franklin, *The History of the Reign of Shah Aulum*, Reprint, Lucknow 1974, pp. 68-70; J.N. Sarkar, *Fall of the Mughal Empire*, Calcutta, 1964, pp.155-157.

35. J.N. Sarkar, 'Delhi during the anarchy 1749-1788 as told in the contemporary Records' in *Indian Historical Records Commission*, Volume III, Calcutta, 1921, p. 4.

36. P.M. Joshi, (ed.), *Persian Records of Maratha History*, Volume II, *Sindhia As Regent of Delhi 1787, 1789-1791*, translation, J.N. Sarkar, Bombay, 1954, pp. 21-22.

37. J.N. Sarkar, *Fall of the Mughal Empire*, Volume III, p. 317.

38. George A. Forster, *Journey from Bengal to England*, pp. 141, 191, 218.

39. W. Franklin, 'An Account of the Present state of Delhi' in *Asiatic Researches*, Volume IV, 1799, p. 426; W. Hamilton, *Description of Hindostan*, Delhi, 1971. (Reprint) Volume I, p. 414.

40. W. Hamilton, *Description of Hindostan*, p. 414.

41. C.A. Bayly, in R.E. Frykenberg, (ed.), *op. cit.*, p. 228.

42. *Ibid.*

43. Zahiruddin Malik, *The Reign of Mohammad Shah*, Bombay, 1977, pp. 342-405.

44. Abul Fazl, *Ain-i-Akbari*, English Translation, Blochmann, New Delhi, 1965, Volume I, p. 37*l*.

45. Mayadharman Sinha, *History of Oriya literature*, New Delhi, 1962, pp.109, 155-162; Sukumar Sen, *History of Bengali Literature*, New Delhi, 1960, pp. 164-168; Annmarie Schimmel, *Sindhi Literature*, Wiesbaden, 1974, pp. 14-19.

46. Abdul Qadir Sarwani, *Urdu ki Adabi Tarikh*, Hyderabad, 1958, p. 59.

47. Maulvi Abdul Haq, *Urdu ki Ibtadai Nashw-o-Numa Men Sufiya-i-Karam Ka Kam*; Aligrah, 1968, p. 76; R.M. Eaton, *Sufis of Bijapur 1300-1700*, New Jersey, 1978, pp. 139-142; T.G. Bailey, *A History of Urdu Literature*, New Delhi, 1979, p. 15.

48. Nasiruddin Hashmi, *Dakhin Men Urdu*, Lucknow, 1963, pp. 74-75, 79-80; Maulvi Abdul Haq, 'Kulliyat-i-Muhammad Quli Qutub Shah, *Urdu*, July 1922, pp. 23-37, quoted in, H.K. Sherwani, *Muhammad Quli Qutub Shah, Founder of Hyderabad*, Bombay, 1967, p. 67.

49. Muhammad Hasan, *Delhi Men Urdu Shairi Ka Tahzibi aur Fikri Pasmanzar*, 2nd edition, Delhi, 1983, pp. 80, 94-95.

50. Shaikh Muhammad Qayamuddin Qayam, *Makhzan-i-Nikat*, Aurangabad, 1929, p. 10.

51. Satish Chandra, 'Cultural and Political Role of Delhi 1675-1725, in Frykenberg, (ed.), *Delhi Through the Ages*, p. 209.

52. Mir Taqi Mir, *Nikatush Shuara*, Delhi, 1972.

53. Ghulam Hamdani Mushafi, *Tazkirah-i-Hindi*, Aurangabad, 1933.

54. Mushafi, *Aqd-i-Suraiya*, Urdu Translation, Alaur Rahman, Patna, 1968.

55. G.S. Srivastava, *Urdu Shairi Ki Irtiqa Men Hindu Shuara ka Hissa*, Allahabad, 1969, pp. 93-95. Some of the well known Hindu Poets were Brindaban Raqam Dehlvi, Raja Naval Raiwafa, Mukundlal, Fidvi Lahori, Lala Lakshmi Narayan Shafiq Aurangabadi.

56. Hatim Zahuruddin, *Diwanzada*, (ed.), Ghulam Husain Zulfiqar, Lahore, 1975, pp. 214-227.

57. *Ibid*. pp. 216-217.

58. Dargah Quli Khan, *Muraqqa-i-Dehli*, Urdu Translation, Nurul Hasan Ansari, Delhi, 1982.

59. Mirza Muhammad Rafi Sauda, *Kulliyat-i-Sauda*, Allahabad, 1971, Volume I, p. 395.

60. Hatim, *Diwanzada*, p. 117.

61. Mir Dard, *Diwan-i-Dard*, Delhi, 1982, p. 90.

62. Sauda, *Kulliyat*, II, p. 72.

63. Mir. *Kulliyat*, I, p. 207.

64. Naim Ahmad, *Shahr Ashob Ka Tahqiqi Mutala*, Aligarh, 1979, pp.19-37.

65. Sauda, *Kulliyat*, I, pp. 226-230; II, pp. 261-266.

66. Mir Taqi Mir, *Zikr-i-Mir*, Urdu Translation Nisar Ahmad Faruqi, as *Mir Ki Ap Biti*, Delhi, 1957, p. 115.

67. Ghulam Husain Tabatabai, *Siyarul Mutakherin*, Urdu Translation, Gokul Prashad, Lucknow, 1874, Volume III, p. 118.

68. Syed Insha Allah Khan Insha, *Dariya-i-Latafat*, Urdu Translation, Pandit Brij Mohan Kaifi, Aurangabad, 1935, pp. 156-159.

69. Murtaza, Husain, *Hadiqatul Aqalim*, Lucknow, 1879, p. 44.

70. Mir, *Mi Ki AP Biti*, p. 174.

71. Archaeological Survey of India, *List of Muhammadan and Hindu Monuments, Delhi Province*, Calcutta, 1919, Volume I, pp. 133;, 167; J.N. Sarkar, *Sindhia As Regent*, p. 27.

72. Mir, *Kulliyat*, I, p. 367.

73. Muhammad Husain Azad, *Ab-i-Hayat*, Allahabad 1980, p. 266.

THE POETS

In any age, only a few can claim greatness in the style of poetry
This age belongs to Mir and Sauda[1]

ایک دو ہی ہوتے ہیں خوش طرز و طور ؎ اب چناں چہ میر و مرزا کا ہے دور

The later Mughal period, barring the political decline of the Mughals, was characterized by an unbroken continuity in the sphere of socio-religious and intellectual activity. It was also the age of the Urdu ghazal and the golden age of Urdu poetry. The contemporary situation, however, not merely brought about a change in the centres of learning and patronage but also cast a constant shadow over the writings of renowned poets from Mir, Sauda and Hatim to Dard and Nazir Akbarabadi. A study of the lives of the poets, their social environment, their outlook and attitudes, prejudices and predilections, serve as vital links in the reconstruction of different facets of 18th century life. In the case of Mir, his sensitiveness to the tragic events in Delhi brought out the best in the tender pathos of the ghazal, expressing deep regret at the passing away of a cherished civilisation. Sauda and to a lesser degree Hatim, reacted with biting sarcasm to the ills of the society while it produced the mystic introversion and indifference to worldly matters in Dard's writings. This sufistic attitude, however, was to a greater or lesser degree shared by all the poets, mysticism being a dominant and almost fashionable form of thought during this period. The last poet, Nazir who had left Delhi before its decline to settle in Agra, reacted to the changing socio-cultural pattern outside court circles by exploring the varied aspects of social environment of Agra.

Mir Taqi Mir 1722-1810

> Do not take my diwan to be a mere collection of verses
> It is an expression of life long experience of suffering and sorrow.[2]

.مجھ کو شاعر نہ کہو میرؔ کہ صاحب میں نے ؂ درد و غم کتنے کیے جمع تو دیوان کیا.

Mir's early life in Akbarabad, his domestic circumstances, his experience in Delhi, the temporary madness and life in Lucknow needs to be critically analyzed for a proper understanding of Mir, the man and his writings. Mir himself has left an account of his life, excluding the last thirty years, in his autobiography Zikr-i-Mir. It does not give his date of birth but the discovery of a manuscript of his poems in the library of Raja of Mahmoodabad.[3] shows that he was born in Akbarabad and died in Lucknow in 1810. Mir belonged to a very poor family, his father Muhammad Ali Mutaqqi, was a darvesh, well known and respected in Akbarabad. Although Mir claimed to be a Syed,[4] most scholars on the basis of available evidence consider him to be a Siddiqi Shaikh.[5] On what basis Mir claimed a Syed lineage is difficult to judge but by the time he wrote Zikr-i-Mir, at the age of sixty he was well known as 'Mir', his poetical title. He had by this time had come to insist on his Syed lineage. One reason could be his desire to claim high parentage to give a further boost to his rising poetical fame. The fact that his claims came to be challenged by his contemporaries is an indication of the social importance attached to one's parentage, race or family connections in the medieval society.

The death of Ali Muttaqi and Amanullah his devoted disciple and Mir's 'uncle' left him a destitute at the tender age of ten or eleven. Mir left his home town and arrived in Delhi in search of a job. Here he was granted a stipend of one rupee a day by Amirul Umara, Samsamuddaulah who held Ali Muttaqi in great reverence. This stipend however stopped because of the death of the Amirulumara during the invasion of Nadir Shah (1739). Mir visited Delhi a second time at the age of seventeen and stayed with Khan Arzu, his step uncle for a number of years. He does not specify the time he spent with him or the education imparted by him. But it is difficult to accept his assertion that he learnt very little from Arzu for he himself refers to him in the Nikat as "his most respected teacher and guide".[6] The influence of Arzu on Mir can hardly be denied as the former had inspired many young poets including Sauda to write in Urdu.[7] Qayam

Chandpuri who lived near Mir's house wrote that for several years he (Mir) acquired knowledge from Arzu.[8] Perhaps Mir's extraordinary pride prevented him from giving recognition to knowledge acquired from Arzu after his estrangement with him. Mir himself is silent on the cause of this estrangement and hostility while it remains a topic of debate among scholars.[9]

Mir started writing in Urdu about 1740-1741 which was also the time when he suffered from temporary madness. His poetic talent came to be appreciated in Delhi to which Mir refers in a number of verses:

> To do him justice, Mir excels in writing verse in Rekhta
> Poets should acknowledge him as Ustad.[10]

ریختہ خوب ہی کہتا ہے جو انصاف کرو ؎ چاہیئے اہلِ سخن میرؔ کو استاد کریں

In an other verse he expresses great pride in the growing popularity of his poetry:

> There is no one who does not carry my diwan with him
> It is a tale of love, why should its fame not be wide spread.[11]

خالی نہیں بغل کوئی دیوان سے مرے ؎ افسانہ عشق کا ہے یہ مشہور کیوں نہ ہو

Like other scholars and poets who comprised the literary elite, Mir was dependent on the patronage of one noble or the other for livelihood. After his estrangement with Khan Arzu he experienced a quick change of patrons for which his own egoism and vanity as well as extreme political instability of the day were responsible. Among his early patrons was Riayat Khan[12] who was closely related to Qamaruddin Khan. Itimadud-daulah II, wazir of the empire from 1724-1748. Another patron of Mir, Khwajah Sara Nawab Bahadur Javed Khan was all powerful in the empire from 1748 to 1752. No eunuch had ever been so exalted before, absolutely illiterate with no administration experience, the nobles revolted at the idea of paying court to such a man and looked down upon him with aristocratic contempt.[13] In spite of the dubious political role, Javed Khan's wealth enabled him to patronize great poets like Mir who is full of appreciation for his kind patron.[14] Patronage of arts, therefore, was no longer the privilege of the noble born but extended to include those who possessed the necessary means. Mir had witnessed the successive palace intrigues between Javed Khan, Safdarjang and finally Imadulmulk who imprisoned and blinded the emperor, Ahmad Shah, yet he is full of praise for Imadulmulk's generosity as a patron of men of learning.[15]

Mir's next patron, Raja Jugal Kishore, wakil of the governors of Bengal Sarfaraz Khan and Alivardi Khan at the court of Muhammad Shah.[16] held the poet in great esteem. But the Raja soon found himself in very hard circumstances and requested Raja Nagar Mal[17] who held the post of *diwan-i-khalisa o Tan*, to take the poet under his protection. The period of peace and comfort did not last beyond a year as Mir was forced to leave Delhi in view of looting of the city by Abdali in 1760 and took shelter in the Jat Kingdom where he met some nobles of Delhi who were living in the Raja's stables. Among them was Azam Khan, the son of Azam Khan the elder who had held a mansab of 6000 under Muhammad Shah. Mir related his woes to him and talked of the happy days.[18]

Soon Mir resumed his connection with his old patron, Raja Nagar Mal, and both decided to stay in the Jat Kingdom. Mir himself explains the reason for his confinement in the Jat kingdom for nearly thirteen years in the Zikr, "Shahjahanabad in those days was little better than wilderness which every six months was laid desolate afresh. In the Jat kingdom there was peace under a prosperous ruler and we settled down under the shadow of his protection.[19] The Jat Kingdom, in fact, served as a refuge to a large number of Delhi literati and nobles, including the ex wazir Imadulmulk, who had been an enemy of the rising Jat State in the years 1753-1754. The Jat ruler, Suraj Mal, though risen from the peasant stock emerged as a patron of men of talent and treated them with the greatest respect.[20] Mir alongwith Raja Nagar Mal attended the darbar of Abdali held after the crushing defeat of the Marathas at Panipat in January 1761. When Abdali left the capital, Nagarmal and Mir returned to Kumber, Mir had again witnessed the destruction of the city and cried over its fate:

Jahanabad now lies in ruins
otherwise there was a house at every step.[21]

اب خرابا ہوا جہاں آباد ہے ورنہ ہر اک قدم پہ یاں گھر تھا

Mir also visited the locality where he had lived and found the place totally deserted:

This time in Delhi, I did not see those friends,
They went away too soon, or Perhaps I arrived too late.[22]

دلّی میں اب کی آکر ان یاروں کو نہ دیکھا ؎ کچھ وے گئے شتابی کچھ ہم بھی دیر آئے

In the same year Mir also visited his native city of Agra after an absence of over twenty two years. The city had not suffered as much material destruction as Delhi but to Mir the city seemed absolutely deserted:

On my return to this city after twenty years
I find a death like silence reigning the city.[23]

شہر میں آیا میں بعد از بست (۲۰) سال ؎ گم تھا یاں سررشتۂ قال و مقال

Mir returned to Delhi with his patron about the time Shah Alam was restored to his ancestral throne with the help of the Marathas in January, 1772. Soon after his arrival in Delhi Mir parted with Nagar Mal due to differences but his association with his son, Bahadur Singh, continued for sometime. Mir's financial condition deteriorated due to the absence of a strong patron and he was forced to beg for benefits from the nobles.[24] A number of verses written around this period express his disappointed and anger at a society which he thought had failed in its duty to provide for him.

On my return to Delhi, I find myself on the brink of starvation
What a wonderful reception greeted me this time![25]

قوت کو پیرانہ سر دلّی میں حیرانی ہوئی ؎ اب کے جو آئے سفر سے خوب مہمانی ہوئی

Mir, in fact, suffered from constant frustration, which was due to his belief that he was not getting his due from society and that his talent remained unappreciated. Here Mir was not wholly justified because in spite of turbulent conditions most of his patrons tried to appreciate the greatness of his art and provide for him accordingly. His patrons before he left for Awadh including Riayat Khan, Raja Jugal Kishore, Raja Nagar Mal and Javed Khan treated him with utmost respect and honour. Even Shah Alam, in spite of his poverty used to occasionally provide for him. The times were so uncertain that with the best of intentions his patrons could do no more than the conditions permitted, Mir's frustration and bad temper became more prominent after 1771 when he returned to Delhi and lived in extreme poverty, By the time he reached Lucknow that had assumed a legendary character.[26] His autobiography, written before his departure from Delhi gives expression to his sense of insecurity, poverty and want repeatedly experienced by him. He also complained of the decline of poetical standards and found very few people of his standing on his return to Delhi after fourteen years. Regarding the state of poetical gatherings in Delhi, they seemed to have lost all their charm for Mir.

Mir had witnessed the fading away of the glories of the Mughals at the centre, the impoverishment of the ruling classes as well as of the monarchy which was in no position to patronize men of talent. In these circumstances Mir keenly desired to go to Lucknow, where already, a large number of poets from Delhi, including Khan Arzu, Sauda and Mir Soz had taken shelter. In 1769 he had written a masnavi on the marriage of Asafuddaulah which, according to scholars, expressed his secret desire to migrate to Lucknow.[27] Mir was invited to come to Lucknow after the death of Sauda in 1781 at the instance of the Nawab's uncle, Salar Jang, who had close relations with Khan Arzu. Mir who had earlier been critical of Arzu's decision to migrate to Awadh[28] reached Lucknow at the age of sixty one and was granted a stipend of rupees three hundred or two hundred[29] a month by the Nawab.

In Lucknow Mir at last found the peace and security he had craved for all his life. Asafuddaulah held Mir in great respect and affection, Mir wrote a number of quasidas and masnavis in his honour though he had very little enthusiasm for this style of poetry. He in fact wrote very few eulogies on his patron, for instance, in the case of Raja Nagar Mal who had been his patron for almost fourteen years, Mir did not write even a single verse in his praise.

Mir lost his stipend under the next Nawab, Wazir Ali, who ruled for only five months which was restored through the good offices of Syed Insha after four years. The incident left Mir very bitter and his dissatisfaction with Lucknow would seem to some scholars a passing phase, especially at a time when he had lost the privileges enjoyed under Asafuddaulah[30] But Mir's dissatisfaction went much deeper than mere financial hardships he had to undergo temporarily. In Lucknow, he did get a respite from poverty and want but he remained dissatisfied with Lucknow's society and found it difficult to adjust to the new environment, its ways and fashions, mannerisms and, above all, its literary and poetical style. Even Urdu language seemed to have undergone a change in Lucknow.[31]

> I wrote verses rich in content and expression
> But few could appreciate my talent[32]

کس کس ادا سے ریختے میں نے کہے ولیک ؎ سمجھا نہ کوئی میری زباں اس دیار میں

The following verse of Mir reflects his unwillingness to come to terms with the superficial glitter of Lucknow's culture rather than dissatisfaction over his temporary troubles:

> Though I have lived in Lucknow for years
> I have been hankering to get away from its society.[33]

برسوں سے لکھنؤ میں اقامت ہے مجھ کو لیک ؎ یاں کے چلن سے رکھتا ہوں عزمِ سفر ہنوز

Mir's dissatisfaction with poetic style and language and culture became more intense as the clientele in Lucknow had narrowed down to the court circles and the courtesan's *Kotha*. The 'Courtesan culture' was ever popular in Delhi in the pre-1757 era but it never acquired the kind of status enjoyed by it in the licentious atmosphere of Lucknow. In Delhi, on the other hand, poetic clientele had a far broader social base which extended from the noblemen to the common man's Khanqah. The affluence of Awadh, its 'new society' of luxury, license, polish and glitter, and little depth, could have little appeal for Mir. He continued to crave for a society however decadent it might appear to outsiders:

> Both my heart and Delhi are desolate
> Yet I find comfort in this deserted city[34]

دل و دلّی دونوں اگر ہیں خراب ؎ پہ کچھ لطف اُس اجڑے گھر میں بھی ہے

By the time Mir arrived in Lucknow his career as a poet had already reached its pinnacle. The bulk of his poetry was written in Delhi when his mental faculties were at their best.[35] Mentally, Mir remained attached to Delhi and its cultural traditions, regardless of the fact that he spent the last thirty years of his life in Lucknow.

It would be incorrect, however, to assume that Mir's view of life was purely sufistic and pessimistic, that he remained absorbed in his own grief and never bothered to "look out of the window". The topic of tragic love is a dominant theme in Mir's poetry but this relates not merely to his personal expriences which culminated in his own disappointment in love, but give expression to the value system of the age. Besides, the greatness and popularity of Mir's poetry did not lie in its sheer melancholia but rather lay in the identification of his personal emotions and experiences with that of his age.

> You lament at your own fate Mir
> Here many great civilizations have risen and fallen.[36]

زیرِ فلک بھلا تو رووے ہے آپ کو میرؔ ؎ کس کس طرح کا عالم یاں خاک ہو گیا ہے

His close association with the nobility and court circles did not prevent him from critically assessing their political role by exposing their disloyalty, selfishness and acts of self aggrandizement at the cost of the empire. It is the deep rooted realism in his verses which appealed to both the elite as well as the common man, the bazaar and the Khanqah:

> Though my verses are appreciated among the select
> I however wish to address myself to common people.[37]

شعر میرے ہیں سب خواص پسند ؎ پر مجھے گفتگو عوام سے ہے

Poetry writing itself, however, as an art, Mir was convinced, was to be confined to the upper classes (*ashraf*) while the lower classes (*ajlaf*) could have no place in it, an attitude which most contemporaries shared with Mir. The rise of the low born was looked upon with suspicion for it threatened the value system and the social order itself. Yet, in spite of these limitations, the desire to know and to explore continued to inspire the society of Mir's times.

Destination seemed in view at every step
But the quest of knowledge urged him to go on.[38]

ہر قدم پر تھی اس کی منزل لیک ؎ سر سے سودائے جستجو نہ گیا

Mirza Sauda (1713-1781)

Sauda, the great contemporary and rival of Mir was born in Delhi to a prosperous merchant of Kabul.[39] His father Mirza Shafi, prospered as a merchant and left a considerable fortune for his son who squandered it away within a short period. Sauda's mother was the daughter of Aurangzeb's *Waqai Nigar*, Niamat Ali Khan who was himself a poet and a critic which gave Sauda the advantage, not merely of an affluent background, but also of close association with the literary and intellectual atmosphere of the age.

The contemporary accounts throw very little light on the early life and career of Sauda. His father had been a successful merchant and most probably his *takhallus* was influenced by his father's profession.[40] It is suggested that Sauda became a mansabdar[41] but this appears to be doubtful. According to Qayam Chandpuri, after exhausting his father's fortune, he became a *musahib*.[42] The possibility of Sauda being given a mansab as a *musahib* can not be ruled out. In any case even if he did become a mansabdar, his career in the official hierarchy could not have lasted for long as no such reference can be found regarding his later life.

Sauda, in keeping with the literary norms of the age, came under the tutelage of Sulaiman Quli Khan[43] and later of Shah Hatim.[44] He also appears to have been greatly influenced by Khan Arzu, though he never formally became his pupil. Sauda started composing verses about 1735, soon achieved popularity and came to be well received in literary circles of Delhi by the early 1740s. Sauda himself speaks of his rising fame with great pride:

My poetry is my only rival
My fame are my verses
My verses, my fame
I the great master of versification Mine the only word that enriches verses.[45]

سخن مرا ہے مقابل مرے سخن کے ہیں ؎ کہ میں سخن سے ہوں مشہور اور سخن مجھ سے
مری زباں ہے ملک سخن میں یک خیاط ؎ عروس معنی کا ہو ٹھیک پیراہن مجھ سے

With Sauda's reputation soaring high he received the patronage of the leading nobles of Delhi. Among his early patrons was an amir of Muhammad Shah's reign Khwaja Sara Basant Khan. During the reign of Ahmad Shah (1748-1754) the Bakshi of Ahdis, Ahmad-Ali Khan Saifuddaulah also seems to have patronized him. He was probably introduced to the court in the reign of Alamgir II when his patron, Imadulmulk held the office of the wazir.

Sauda's career reached its peak around this time. He did probably more than any poet to raise the status of Urdu as a literary language, for despite the zeal of his predecessors the attitude to Urdu in high literary circles was at best one of tolerance, Sauda along with Mir and Dard raised it to the status enjoyed by Persian. The popularity of Sauda has led many scholars to believe that he was granted the title of poet laureate but the evidence supplied by them is not authentic.[46] Similarly the incident of Sauda's refusal to accept the title from emperor Shah Alam II is not valid as no other contemporary writer has recorded it.[47]

Recognition of fame alone could not free the poet from the hazards of earning a living. Sauda continued to live in Delhi as long as he received the patronage of one patrons or the other. Many leading poets, including Khan Arzu, Qayam and others had already left the capital. With the exception of Mir, Sauda was the last leading poet to leave Delhi being a witness to the repeated ravaging of the city at the hands of the Marathas and later by Ahmad Shah Abdali (1757). In the *Mukhammas Shehr Ashob*, Sauda is overwhelmed by the catastrophic downfall of the city of Delhi.[48] In the *Tazhik-i-Rozgar*,[49] which is apparently a merry skit on an impoverished noblemen and his horse, is also full of side lights on the political decline at the capital, while the half dead horse is symbolic of the empire in the last throes of its fall.[50]

Sauda left Delhi and reached Farrukhabad with his patron, Imadulmulk, who had been ordered by Abdali to collect revenue from the province of Awadh. The diwan of Nawab Ahmad Khan Bangash, Meherban Khan, requested Imadulmulk to leave Sauda under his protection.[51] It was during this time that Sauda received an invitation from Nawab Shujauddaulah to come to Faizabad. But the poet is said to have politely declined the offer saying he was not lacking in comfort under his current patron:

> O Sauda, running after worldly goods
> Is nothing but a futile exercise,
> For even if one acquired them

Life is too short to enjoy the material gains. [52]

سودا پے دنیا تو بہر سو کب تک ؎ آوارہ ازیں کوچہ باں کو کب تک
حاصل یہی اس سے ہے کہ دنیا ہووے ؎ بالفرض ہوا یوں بھی تو پھر تو کب تک

It was the death of Ahmad Khan Bangash in 1771 and the consequent decline in the fortunes of his patron that forced Sauda to leave Farrukhabad for Faizabad. Shujauddalah welcomed Sauda's decision to migrate to his capital but also subtly reminded the poet of the couplet he had previously sent, declining to come to Faizabad. Sauda was offended and withdrew from the court till the accession of Asafuddaulah in 1775.[53]

In Lucknow, Sauda continued to command respect and popularity although financially he did not seem to be satisfied with his position. A grant of a jagir yielding Rs. 6,000 annually was later bestowed upon Sauda after his quarrel with Fakhir Makin, a leading poet of Persian.[54] Despite the life of comparative ease and affluence, Sauda keenly yearned for Delhi, a characteristic he shared with Mir, though with less intensity:

Adversity forced Sauda to leave his home town
He has been a homeless wanderer since long.[55]

سودا وطن کو تج کر گردش سے آسماں کے ؎ آوارۂ غریبی ہے اتنی مدتوں سے

Sauda's poetry has often been compared with the works of his great contemporary, Mir. The two are considered by critics to be antithetical poets, while Mir's verses are full of pathos, it is pointed out, those of Sauda evoke spontaneous applause. These characteristics continued to inspire poets of a later generation.[56] The description seems to be rather superficial. In fact both were born poets and great rivals:

O Sauda do not recite this ghazal before Mir
What does he knew of this form and style of poetry.[57]

نہ پڑھیو یہ غزل سودا تو ہرگز میر کے آگے ؎ وہ ان طرزوں سے کیا واقف وہ یہ انداز کیا سمجھے

Both were masters of their trade, and lived in Delhi, but their social background and material conditions differed widely, also their nature and inevitably their poetic style. Mir having risen from the lower rungs of society lived in poverty for a long time, his sufferings being exceptional. His poem '*darhajv Khana-i-khud*' may be noticed in this context. The chiefly quality of his poetry did not lie merely in the tragic theme of the ghazal but in its realism which may be ascribed to his peculiar personal circumstances as well as his milieu, hence he more than Sauda is predisposed to reflect the distress he saw around himself. Sauda also faced the vicissitudes of times but coming from an affluent background did not suffer the kind of privations experienced by Mir. He therefore appears more as a spectator and a critic rather than as a sufferer like Mir.

Although, Sauda was fond of elaborate form, using difficult rhymes and high sounding words the topic of tender love and many other varied aspects of life find expression in his poetry. The political and economic insecurity of his day, the reflections of old age, the futility of life and its lost opportunities are expressed, in spite of all his apparent high spirits in the sufistic style adopted by other poets of his times.

Shah Hatim (1699-1791)

Shaikh Zahuruddin Hatim was the most well known of the early fathers of Urdu poetry and also the founder, along with Naji and Abru, of the Delhi school of poets. Very little information is available about Hatim's ancestors, early life and education, even his name has not been correctly given by most Tazkirah writers.[58] Born in Delhi in 1699 his father, Shaikh Fatahuddin, was employed in the army and Hatim too joined the same profession.[59] The claim of some writers that he always led a carefree and comfortable life is difficult to accept[60] because a number of verses written in 1723 indicate Hatim's plight and his search for a suitable job. He also wrote a long *Shahr Ashob*, a decade before the invasion of Nadir Shah in which he criticized the political and social ills of Muhammad Shah's reign. His tone is clearly marked by worldly bitterness although later he seems to have adopted the ideals of contentment, out of conviction or as a result of the impact of the contemporary situation on his mind.

O Hatim do not fall into the trap of high office and jagir
Waste not your life in greed for palaces.[61]

دام سے منصب و جاگیر کے باز آ حاتمؔ   یہ دمِ نقد نہ کھو ذکرِ محالات کے بیچ

Most tazkirah writers, with the exception of Mir, who dismisses him as an egotistical fool and his poetry as lacking in rhyme,[62] praise Hatim's talent.[63] Hatim himself refers to the disrespect shown to him by Mir in a couplet written in 1775.

> That youngster, is like the Mir of the game of cards.
> That changes hands frequently.[64]

تھا ابھی ہم پاس ابھی جاتا رہا غیروں کے پاس ؎ آشنائی میں وہ لڑکا گنجفے کا میر ہے

Hatim was perhaps overshadowed by the skill and talent shown by younger poets like Mir, who like many other poets had been a follower of Hatim but later left the old *ustad* in view of his jealousy towards Sauda who was also Hatim's pupil.

Among the important patrons of Hatim may be mentioned the name of Umdaul Mulk, Nawab Amir Khan Anjam.[65] He is said to have given himself to wine bibbing in his company and was considerably influenced by the wit and intellectuality of Anjam. He also attached himself to Nuruddaulah Fakhir Khan[66] during the absence of Anjam who served as subehdar of Allahabad from 1742-1745. During these years, Hatim's poetry had become popular both among the elite as well as the common people. Interestingly against the contemporary practice, Hatim unlike Mir and Sauda, did not compose any qasida in praise of any of his patrons, only occasional verses in their praise, including one on Alamgir II and Zabita Khan,[67] can be found in the diwanzada. The nobles continued to appreciate Hatim's talent even after he become a recluse while the poet in turn never failed to appreciate their generosity.

In spite of maintaining contacts with the nobles, Hatim never went back from the sufistic path he had adopted. He came to live with his *Pir*, Shah Badal Ali,[68] who bestowed on his devotee (*murid*) the rosary, prayer carpet and *Khirqa* and initiated him into the Suhrawardi *tariqa*. After Shah Badal's death, Hatim spent most of his time in Shah Taslim's Khanqah, situated near Rajghat.[69] Muhammad Hussain Azad refers to Shah Taslim as a pious sufi poet who was visited by a number of poets.[70] Similar information is given by Saadatyar Khan.[71] A number of verses written in the last years of Hatim's life only confirm his faith in his *Pir*.

> Kings lean on the throne and crown for support
> For a darvesh the doorstep of his Pir is support enough.[72].

بادشاہوں کو ہے گر تخت و چتر کا تکیہ ؎ ہے فقیروں کے تئیں پیر کے در کا تکیہ

Hatim's personality compares favourably with Mir Dard's in many respects. Hatim in his youth was a happy-go-lucky man possessing the characteristics of a young gentlemen of Muhammad Shah's reign,[73] well to do. appreciating good company, good poetry — a man of the world. Mir Dard too in early days aspired to enter royal service like any ambitious youth of his age. Yet both of them adopted asceticism, lived in Delhi, saw its changing fortunes with patience and fortitude instead of leaving the city in search of shelter and patrons. Dard's task was perhaps easier as he had inherited the sufistic attitude while Hatim had to find his way to it through his various *pirs*. Both of them never severed relations with the world at large, surrounded by friends and pupils, participated in poetical gatherings held in Shah Taslim's Khanqah. Hatim also regularly visited Mushafi's poetical gatherings.[74] The account of Hatim's life and attitudes may be concluded in his own words, expressing the typical sufistic attitude of his times.

> We had a good time in this world Hatim,
> God know what will befall us in the life to come.[75]

دنیا میں تو خوب گذری حاتم ؛ عقبیٰ میں بھی دیکھئے خدا ہے

Khwajah Mir Dard (1719-1785)

Mir Dard, the great mystic poet traced his lineage to the family of mystics for he was descended on his father's side from Khwajah Bahauddin Naqshband and on the mother's side from Hazrat Ghaus-i-Azam, Abdul Qadir Gilani. Dard's father Muhammad Nasir claimed to have been blessed in 1734 by a vision of the prophet's grandson, Iman Hasan, who introduced him to the secret of the true Muhammadan path. Dard became his father's disciple and spent the rest of his life propagating the doctrine of the Tariqa-i-Muhammadi of the Naqshbandis. Although Dard had earlier joined the imperial service he gave it up to lead the life of a darvesh and devoted himself to study and meditation.

Dard's family lived near Paharganj outside Shahjahanabad, later known as Baraf Khana. During the sack of Delhi 1739, Aurangzeb's daughter, Mihr Parwar Begum offered shelter to Nasir's family. But the mystics turned down the offer in spite of the state of anarchy and violence in the city in the sufi tradition of trust in the 'mercy of God'. Later the sufis accepted the renewed offer and the princess built a house for them in Kucha Chelan. Dard advised his followers not to associate themselves with the rich but uninvited callers were to be welcomed. The sufis could also accept gifts such as *madad-i-mash* grants provided they were offered unconditionally.[76] In his youth, writes Firaq, Dard asked the emperor Muhammad Shah not to disturb him by his visits though later he did not mind the presence of Shah Alam II in his musical gatherings.[77]

Dard was not only a great mystic but a poet of distinction as well who wrote on philosophic and mystic themes. To Dard poetry was an instrument of self-revelation and not means of earning a livelihood by writing odes in praise of patrons and satires on one's opponents. His love poetry is intermingled with mystical love, describing the power of love in terms of obedience to God, prophet and the Imams, sweeping away reasons and intellect aside.[78] The vanity and reality of life, its joys and sorrows, the greatness of man in the hierarchy of life, contentment and resignation are the important themes of Dard's mystical poetry. He became the undisputed master of mystical Urdu poetry, perhaps the only poet who achieved a complete blending of mysticism and verse.[79]

Following his father's example, he participated in the assemblies of poets which were frequently held in Delhi. He also studied poetry with Khan Arzu the aristotle of Urdu literature for some time. Mir was on friendly terms with Dard and attended the mushairas that later came to be held at Dard's house, twice a month. Dard could boast of a number of disciples. These included Qayam Chandpuri (d. 1795) who was one of the best ghazal writers of the age. Mushafi too met Dard several times before migrating to Lucknow. Among his followers were Hindus like Laxmi Narayan Shafiq for whom meeting Dard was "something like worship". Dard was certainly conscious of his growing fame which finds expression in a number of verses.[80]

> I do not look for mere applause for my poetry.
> It should suffice if critics bear witness to the excellence of my verses.[81]

نخواہم در واز تحسین کس اثبات حقیقت ؎ کلام من بود بس در سخن فہماں گواہ من

Dard though a mystic was not hostile to earthly love and beauty and it would be futile to brand his love lyrics as 'mystical'.

Flowers and orchids do not interest me.

The garden has no charm for me without the beloved.[82]

گل وگلزار خوش نہیں آتا ؛ باغ بے یار خوش نہیں آتا

Dard continued to reside in Delhi at a time when the city was repeatedly devastated and witnessed the exodus of a large number of poets and sufis including Shah Abdul Aziz and Mirza Mazhar who took shelter with the Rohillas for some time. Yet in true sufistic attitude he was able to withstand the upheaval with great patience and equanimity. Although he spoke very little about these afflictions in his spirituals diaries or *risalas*, he refers to the fate of Delhi in a number verses:

Delhi which has fallen on evil times and laid waste,
Now tears flow instead of rivulets,
This city was once like the face of the beloved
And its suburbs were like the down on the cheek of the youth.[83]

دہلی کہ خراب کردہ اکنوں دہرش ؛ جاری شدہ اشکہا بجائے نہرش
بودست این شہر مثل روئے خوباں ؛ چوں خط بتاں بود سوادِ شہرش

In spite of his apparent detachment from worldly matters, Dard could not wholly remain so. He was deeply pained at the sufferings of the people of Delhi which finds expression in his diaries: "The tale of their woes is so grim that I feel myself buried alive with grief".[84]

Dard also noted the weakness of the rulers of his day, the negligence of army officers (mansabdars) and a general decline in moral standards. He advised the economically deprived to face their problems with patience and fortitude, to have trust in God for it was a time when even the rich were in desperate circumstances.[85] On the whole however Dard preferred to remain silent on the terrible events in Delhi in the Naqshbandi tradition of *Khalwat dar Anjuman* i.e. seclusion in the multitude yet this silence itself was an expression of grief and helplessness regarding the life and politics of the age and represented the view point of a significant section of society.

Nazir Akbarabadi (1735-1830)

Wali Muhammad, poetically called Nazir Akbarabadi was a poet with a difference and cannot be classed with any particular school of poetry of his age. Born in Delhi in 1735 Nazir was a contemporary of Mir, Sauda and Dard as well as of the Lucknow poets including Insha, Jurat and Nasikh. His style of poetry however cannot be said to belong to either Delhi or Lucknow school in view of his detachment from the literary ideals of the day. Contemporary tazkirah writers failed to recognize his talent or include him among the great poets of the times since his verses were "On the tongues of the people of the market".[86] Muhammad Husain Azad, the first literary historian of Urdu poetry in his monumental work did not take any serious notice of the poet[87] though almost all the characteristics he sought in Urdu poetry are found in Nazir's writings in abundance. His poetic genius came to be recognized only later, with the weakening of old conventions in Urdu poetry.[88]

Nazir broke away not merely from the formal conventionlism of poetic style but also from the pattern of life followed by the literati and intellectuals of the age by refusing to depend on the patronage of the noblemen, including the Raja of Bharatpur and the Nawab of Awadh.[89] The family of Nazir left for Agra, when he was still a youth, where he settled down to lead the life of an ordinary school teacher. He was also later engaged as tutor to the six children of Raja Bilas Rai. He had a life long association with the Raja and his sons and it was mostly due to their endeavours that his poetry could be preserved for posterity.

Agra like Delhi was a great centre of literary activity and the hometown of great poets like Mir. Besides, Urdu, Braj poetry was also popular in Agra in view of its proximity to Mathura. The contention that Nazir's language was the local Urdu dialect of Agra which came to be polished by the poets of Delhi and Lucknow[90] seems unacceptable as Nazir had attained manhood in Delhi, and learnt his language as spoken in Delhi before he left for Agra. The free use of Hindi and Brajbhasha in his poetry, however may be ascribed to the local influences in Agra. Among his followers and pupils, tazkirah writers mention the names of Qutubuddin Batin, who compiled a tazkirah *Gulistan-i-BeKhizan* in defence of Nazir against a critical assessment of his master by Shefta.[91] Raja Balwant Singh, son of Raja Chet Singh of Benaras, Shaikh Husain Bakshi and many others were included among his pupils.[92]

Nazir's religion has been a subject of controversy. His father was a sunni but he himself adopted shia faith, probably due to the influence of his mother who was a Shia by faith. Religious bigotry was not part of his nature and though himself a Shia was broadminded enough to be a great admirer of mystics including Shah Fakharuddin of Delhi[93] and compose numerous poems on Hindu Gods including one in praise of Lord Krishna.[94] After his death Shia and Sunni Muslims and Hindus laid claims on his mortal remains. Both the Muslims sects prayed at his funeral in their respective manner while the Hindus carried away the sheet of cloth that covered his dead body.[95]

Nazir like his famous contemporary poets, Mir Sauda and Dard belongs to the transitionary age, political as well as cultural. The dissolution of the empire and the weakening of the old ruling groups was accompanied by a steady emergence of indigenous cultural trends. The new political groups were not essentially Persianised and spoke the language of their respective regions while Urdu seemed to be fast rivalling Persian as the vehicle of expression to the extent that the Mughal emperor Shah Alam II started writing poetry in Urdu. No where else was the thrust of indigenous elements more evident than in Nazir's poetry though the same trends are also noticeable in the poetry of Hatim, Sauda and Mir. His break with the patronage system and dis-association with Persian culture contributed to Nazir's triumph. It heralded an era of new cultural traditions in which Sauda and Mir had barely made some inroads.

Nazir was certainly the most "unaccountable" figure in the poetry of his age[96]wholly detached from the literary ideals of his times. The local colour in Nazir's poetry has drawn the attention of all critics, whereas other poets wrote occasionally on nature, festivals and domestic animals, it is Nazir who passionately brought out the beauty of men and nature in his poetry.[97]

Undoubtedly, Nazir made a definite departure from the traditional style of poetry which was a significant change, but more important was the innate poetic worth of his poetry.[98] The variety of themes offered by Nazir in simple language reveals him as the poet of the people happily sharing their lives, their moments of joy and sorrow. The absence of court influences because of the decline of political importance of Agra must have also helped him in the portrayal of the life of a common man in Agra personified in the person of Nazir himself:

> Call Nazir by any name, a lover, a prisoner or a mullah
> A writer, a begger or a poet, he belongs to Agra.[99]

عاشق کہو اسیر کہو آگرے کا ہے ۔ ملا کہو دبیر کہو آگرے کا ہے
مفلس کہو فقیر کہو آگرے کا ہے ۔ شاعر کہو نظیر کہو آگرے کا ہے

Nazir's writings present a refreshing response to the "time of troubles", instead of expressing a sense of nostalgia or frustration for the world that was no more, he faced the challenge of the age by exploring the present and by seeking inspiration for his poetry from the common man.

NOTES

1. Mir Taqi Mir, *Kulliyat*, II, p. 134.
2. *Ibid.*, I, p. 443.
3. Abdul Bari Asi (ed) *Kulliyat-i-Mir*, Lucknow, 1941, p. 7
4. Mir, *Mir Ki Ap Biti*, pp. 29, 31, 87, gives his father's name as Mir Muhammad Ali, his own name as Mir Muhammad Taqi and his son's as Mir Faiz Ali.
5. Qayam Chand Puri, *Makhzan-i-Nikat*, Aurangabad, 1929, p. 40 Mir Hasan, *Tazkirah-i-Shuara-i-Urdu*, Aligarh, 1922, p. 34.
6. Mir Taqi Mir, *Nikatush Shuara*, P. 25.
7. Saadat Khan Nasir, *Tazkirah-i-Khushmarka-i-Zeba*, Lahore, 1970, Vol. I, p. 140.
8. Qayam Chandpuri, *Makhzan-i-Nikat*, p. 41; Qudratullah Qasim *Majmua-i-Naghz*, 1973, Vol. II, p. 230.
9. Muhammad Husain Azad, *Ab-i-Hayat*, p. 203; Asi, *Kulliyat-i-Mir*, p.17; Nisar Ahmad Faruqi, *Talaash-i-Mir*, New Delhi, 1974, p. 85.
10. Mir, *Kulliyat*, I, p. 140.
11. *Ibid.*, p. 166
12. Shah Nawaz Khan, *Maasirul Umarah*, Translation Beni Prasad and H. Beveridge, Patna, 1979, Part II, Volume II, pp. 608-609; Mir, *Zikr-i-Mir*, p. 98.
13. J.N. Sarkar, *Fall of the Mughal Empire*, New Delhi, 1971, Volume II, pp. 209-211, 233-234.
14. Mir, *Mir Ki Ap Biti*, p. 103.
15. *Ibid.*, p. 152
16. Zahiruddin Malik, *The Reign of Muhammad Shah*, p. 144.
17. J.N. Sarkar, *Fall of the Mughal Empire*, Volume II, p. 16.
18. Mir, *Mir ki Ap Biti*, p. 130
19. *Ibid.*, p. 133
20. J.N. Sarkar, *Fall of the Mughal Empire*, Volume, II, p. 325.
21. Mir, *Kulliyat*, I, p. 64.
22. *Ibid.*, p. 193
23. Mir, *Kulliyat*. II, p, 132.
24. Mir, *Mir Ki Ap Biti*, p. 162
25. *Ibid.*, I, p. 395.
26. Muhummad Husain Azad, *Ab-i-Hayat*, pp. 206-207; Fateh Ali Gardizi, *Tazkirah-i-Rekhta Goyan*, Aurangabad 1933, p. 138; Hakim Qudratullah Shauq, *Majmua-i-Naghz*, Volume II, pp. 230-231.
27. Jamil Jalibi, *Muhammad Taqi Mir*, Delhi, 1983, p. 32; Gian Chand Jain, *Urdu Masnavi Shimali Hind Men*, Aligarh, 1969, p. 241
28. Mir, *Mir Ki Ap Biti*, pp. 109-110
29. Mirza Lutf, *Gulshan-i-Hind*, Lahore, 1906, p, 210. Bhagwandas Hindi, *Safina i-Hindi*, Patna, 1958, p. 205

30. Safdar Ah, *Mir Aur Miryat*, Bombay, 1972, pp. 139-141; Kazim Ali Khan, 'Mir Aur Lucknow', *Ajkal*, March, 1984, pp. 85-86

31. Syed Insha, *Dariya-i-Latafat*, pp. 67-68, 104-105; A. Sharar, *Guzashta Lucknow*, New Delhi, 1971, pp. 129-131

32. Mir, *Kulliyat*, I, p. 502

33. *Ibid.*, p. 659.

34. *Ibid.*, p. 496.

35. Safdar Ah, *Mir Aur Miryat*, pp. 204-205, Mir completed the first two diwans in Delhi. The third contains verses written both in Delhi and Lucknow, the fourth diwan was written after the death of Asafuddaulah when he lost his stipend. The fifth and sixth were written in the last ten or fifteen years of his life. But the first two diwans contain larger number of verses, about 7,700 while the last four written in Lucknow contain only 2,184 verses.

36. Mir, *Kulliyat*, I, p. 247.

37. *Ibid.*, 438

38. Mir, *Kulliyat*, I, p. 37.

39. For a detailed discussion Sauda's ancestors see Shaikhchand, *Sauda*, Aurangabad, 1936, pp. 35-36; Khaliq Anjum, *Mirza Rafi Sauda*, Aligarh, 1966, pp. 66-72

40. Muhammad Hasan, *Mutala-i-Sauda*, Lucknow, 1965, p. 7.

41. Khwajah Khan Hamid Aurangabadi, *Tazkirah-i-Gulshan-i-Guftar*, Lucknow, 1963, p. 60

42. Qayam Chandpuri, *Makhzan-i-Nikat*, p. 35.

43. Muhammad Husain Azad, *Abi-Hayat*, p. 149

44. *Ibid.*

45. Sauda, *Kulliyat*, II, p. 95

46. Khaliq Anjum, *Mirza Rafi Sauda*, pp. 86-90.

47. Muhammad Husain Azad, *Abi-i-Hayat*, pp. 149-50, Mir and Qayam do not give details or the name of the persons who conferred the title on Sauda.

48. Sauda *Kulliyat-i-Sauda*, II, pp. 261-266.

49. *Ibid.*, pp. 230-234.

50. *Ibid.*

51. Qayam Chandpuri, *Makhzan-i-Nikat*, p. 55.

52. Sauda, *Kulliyat*, II, p. 151.

53. Muhammad Husain Azad, *Ab-i-Hayat*, p. 151.

54. *Ibid.*

55. Sauda, *Kulliyat*, II, p. 132

56. Amir Minai, *Diwan-i-Amir Minai*, Lucknow, 1942, p. 148.

57. Sauda, *Kulliyat*, II, p. 126.

58. Mir, *Nikat ush Shuara*, p. 79; Mir Hasan, *Tazkirah*, p. 78; Laxmi Narayan Shafiq, *Chamanistan-i-Shuara*, Aurangabad, 1929, p. 134, refers to him as 'Shaikh Muhammad Hatim'. But Qudratullah Qasim, *Majmua-i-Naghz*, Vol. I, p. 180, and Mustafa Khan Shefta, *Gulshan-i-Bekhar*, Urdu Translation, Karachi, 1963, p. 71 give his correct name.

59. Ghulam Hamdani Mushafi, *Aqd-i-Suraiya*, Urdu Tr., Alaur Rehman, Patna, 1968, p. 21.

60. Mushafi, *Tazkirah-i-Hindi*, p. 80.

61. Hatim, *Diwanzada*, p. 85

62. Mir, *Nikat*, p. 77.

63. Gardezi *Tazkirah-i-Rekhta Goyan*, p. 49, Qayam, *Makhzan*, p. 24.

64. Hatim, *Diwanzada*, p. 118.

65. *Ibid.*, p. 41.

66. *Ibid.*, p. 42.

67. *Ibid.*, p. 170

68. *Ibid.*, p. 88; Mir Badal Ali Shah was one of the popular sufi saints during the reign of Muhammad Shah whose Khanqah near Qadam Sharif was frequently visited by poets including Hatim, see Muhammad Husain Azad *Ab-i-Hayat*, p. 113.

69. Qasim, *Majmua-i-Naghz*, I, p. 180.

70. Muhammad Husain Azad, *Abi-i-Hayat*, p. 114.

71. Saadat Yar Khan, *Majalis-i-Rangin*, (ed.) Syed Masud Hasan Rizvi, Lucknow, 1929, p. 3.

72. Hatim, *Diwanzada*, p. 178.

73. Muhammad Husain Azad, *Ab-i-Hayat*, p. 113.

74. Mushafi, *Tazkirah-i-Hindi*, p. 80.

75. Hatim, *Diwanzada*, p. 179.

76. Mir Dard, *Ilmul Kitab*, Delhi, 1892, pp. 521-524.

77. Nasir Firaq, *Maikhana-i-Dard*, Delhi, 1925, p. 121.

78. Annmarie Schimmel, *Pain and Grace*, Lieden 1976, pp. 64-65.

79. *Ibid.*

80. Mir Dard, *Diwan*, p., 35.

81. Mir Dard, *Risail-i-Araba-i-Dard, Nala-i-Dard*, Bhopal, p. 38.

82. Mir Dard, *Diwan*, p. 30; also, pp. 31, 65, 78, 90.

83. Mir Dard, *Nala-i-Dard*, p. 20.

84. Mir Dard, *Dard-i-Dil*, p. 181.

85. Mir Dard, *Ilmulkitab*, pp. 241-245.

86. Mustafa Khan Shefta, *Gulshan-i-Bekhar*, p. 320.

87. Muhammad Husain Azad, *Ab-i-Hayat*, p. 94.

88. Abdul Ghafoor Shahbaz, *Zindagani-i-Benazir*, (ed.) Muhammad Husain, New Delhi, 1981; Also see, Makhmoor Akbarabadi, *Roohi-i-Nazir*, Lucknow, 1978; Salim Jafar, (ed.), *Gulzar-i-Nazir*, Allahabad, 1951; 'Nigar', Lucknow, 1940, *Nazir Number*, Articles by Majrooh Gorakhpuri and Syed Ahtesham Husain.

89. Abdul Ghafoor Shahbaz. *Zindagani-i-Benazir*, pp. 140-141.

90. Makhmoor Akbarabadi, *Roohi Nazir*, p. 30.

91. Abdul Ghafoor Shahbaz, *Zindagani-i-Benazir*, p. 175.

92. *Ibid.*, p. 181.

93. *Ibid.*, 157, 162-164.

94. Nazir Akbarabadi, *Kulliyat-i-Nazir*, Allahabad, 1976, pp. 55-96.

95. Shahbaz, *Nazir Akbarabadi*, p. 135.

96. Muhammad Sadiq, *History of Urdu Literature*, p. 163.

97. Nazir, *Kulliyat*, 295.

98. Muhammad Hasan, *Nazir Akbarabadi*, New Delhi, 1973, p. 43.

99. Nazir, *Kulliyat*, p. 340.

3

THE MONARCHY

Those who once ruled over vast territories before our eyes
None wants to even utter the names of those kings now.[1]

ہمارے دیکھتے زیرِ نگیں تھا ملک سب جن کے　　　کوئی اب نام بھی لیتا نہیں ان ملک گیروں کا

The monarchy, like other medieval institutions which had reached its culmination in the seventeenth century, was transformed from its pivotal position in the state to one of dependence and subordination in terms of actual power by the middle of the eighteenth century. The decline of the empire notwithstanding, constitutionally, the Mughal emperor remained the supreme head of the political system while every aspirant to political power continued to seek legitimacy in his name. The last two decades of the century witnessed this keen competition among the contending powers transform into a struggle to control the emperor's person as well. The authority of the Mughal crown virtually ended with the acceptance of British protection by Shah Alam II in 1803 although the fiction of Mughal authority continued to be maintained till the revolt in 1857.

In view of the absence of any formal exposition on the concept of monarchy pertaining to this period, Urdu poetry, especially the *qasidas*[2] written in praise of the emperors and nobles, besides demonstrating the poet's complete command over the language and the rhetoric device are an extremely valuable source for estimating the position of monarchy within the framework of the late medieval Indian concept of government and society. The eulogization of the emperors, from Muhammad Shah to royal weaklings like Alamgir II and Shah Alam II, need not be dismissed as mere samples of unbridled sycophancy. They highlight the survival of the concept of royal legitimacy associated with the Mughal monarchy in the eighteenth century. The emperor remained the legitimate source of all power, a special creature as well as the shadow of God fulfilling the 'social needs' of the society.[3] The king who occupied the throne only through the will of God to protect and guide his subjects deserved to be praised by the poets.

Sauda's qusidas on the contemporary Mughal emperor Alamgir II[4] and the heir apparent, Prince Ali Gauhar[5] give expression to contemporary attitudes towards the Mughal rulers in an age marked by the decline of their political authority. Sauda's awareness of such a decline is clear in one of his verses in which he laments that a person (Mughal dynasty), whose rule once extended to twenty two subahs, is now unable to control even Koil.[6]

The knowledge of the decline the empire and the royal authority, however, did not prevent Sauda or Mir from writing qasidas on the contemporary emperors. The praise showered on the kings by the poets, though forming an essential characteristic of the conventional style of poetry also highlight the prevailing political and social attitudes vis-a-vis the Mughal monarchy. The Mughal empire had virtually disintegrated when Sauda and Mir wrote these eulogies, but Mughal rule had not been replaced by that of a new dynasty or a new system of government. The emperor continued to enjoy the status of the nominal sovereign authority in India[7] although the dominion of the house of Timur existed only as a mere peagent to preserve appearances, and served the purpose of any successful usurper of the authority and possessions of the empire.

The poets like many medieval thinkers both inside the court and outside it, who justified monarchy in spite of its unislamic nature, on the ground of social necessity,[8] support monarchical rule as the only form of government capable of ensuring the stability of the state. This attitude is not confined to court historians like Barani or Abul Fazl but is precisely the attitude of the medieval Hindi poets[9] who had little connection with court life, thus reflecting a wide and popular acceptance of this concept of sovereignty in medieval India. Sauda, in one of his qasidas on the emperor Alamgir II, elevates the status of the emperor, in keeping with the medieval tradition to the position of God's representative on earth.[10]

The very presence of the monarch, points out Sauda, is a sufficient reason for his subjects to obey him.[11] He is held in such universal awe and fear that even bubbles in the sea would turn into the eggs of *huma* to pay homage to the king if he went sailing for pleasure.[12] Sauda shows preference not only for the Mughal dynasty and monarchy which traditionally served as the symbol of social stability among diverse social groups, from the landlords to the Ulema and traders[13] but also expected the emperors to fulfil this role with a sense of justice and use of military power. Sauda expresses his admiration for the Mughal monarchy in different idioms and similes:

> O king, thy lineage has attained the height of the Sun
> None of the seven skies can ever touch such heights.[14]

شہا جو نسب تیرا آفتاب کو پہنچا ؛ ہر آسمان نے پہنچی نکی ہے آسماں پہ کلاہ

Again, while praising Alamgir II's good deeds and personal qualities, Sauda also eulogizes his royal lineage by comparing it to the high position of the Sun in the cosmos. Similarly, Ali Gauhar's prestige and honourable position, according to the poet reaches such heights of glory that it seems as if his throne has been placed in the *Burj-i-hamal*, the constellation of aries, which seems to get illuminated by the mere presence of the king. In another verse, the poet lays stress on the protective role of the emperor and prays for a long and prosperous reign:

> As your majesty is the protector of the world
> All eyes are turned towards you for succour,
> May your dignity and honour last till the day of judgement
> And Shah Alam may continue to illuminate the universe like the
> Sun.[15]

شاہا تری طرف ہے نگاہِ عالم ؎ ازبس تری ذات ہے پناہِ عالم
قائم رہے تا حشر ترا جاہ و جلال ؎ روشن جوں آفتاب شاہِ عالم

The eulogization of the Mughal emperors by Sauda can be further noted in his frequent utilization of some of the traditional symbols of royalty such as the *huma* to connote their real or supposed glory.[16] (According to Persian tradition if the shadow of a *huma* (eagle) falls on a person, he attains royalty) Sauda's verses point to the survival of many royal prerogatives such as the *chatr* and *Darbash*, that is royal parasol and baton, that had taken shape during the Sultanate[17] period and had been further elaborated during the Mughal rule.[18] A large huma was usually marked on a parasol in gold which shaded the monarch under its wings as an auspicious omen.

While expressing admiration for the Mughal emperors and pinning his faith in their rule, Sauda does not forget to highlight the duties of an ideal king. According to him a good ruler is one who works for the welfare of his subjects, giving priority to the king's duty of administering justice without discriminating between the high and the low and extending his patronage to the ascetics.[19] He is also the destroyer of all evil elements and is the protector of the weak and the needy:

> O! Protector of the world and embodiment of justice
> God forbid, that any evil doer dare oppress any of your subjects.
> Even if a moth is burnt in the course of your justice
> The candle does not escape retribution, burning itself out at dawn.[20]

> جہاں پناہ ترے درگہہ عدالت میں ؎ کسی کو دیوے اذیت کوئی معاذاللہ
> جلے جو شام کو پروانہ بزم میں تیرے ؎ تو صبح شمع کے آتا ہے سر پہ روزِ سیاہ

In his state, therefore, no one dares to harm anyone, even if a man dies a natural death the authorities are subjected to explain the cause of his death in the same manner as a candle that suffers (burns) throughout the night, is blamed in the morning for the death of a moth.[21] Sauda further elaborates on the importance of the duty of a ruler to protect his kingdom against enemies with an interesting simile: the shining black handle of his sword proclaims a "black day" to all his enemies.[22] No enemy of the state can withstand the onslaught of the emperor's anger and power for long: the enemies disappear just as the pages of a book might be blown away by strong wind.[23]

Sauda lays great emphasis on the paternal role of the rulers. He compares a kingdom to a garden and subjects to flowers, the king being as beneficial to the people as clouds are to the garden.[24] The poet appeals to the emperor as the final authority to redress the grievances of the subjects saying that it is by the grace of his majesty's goodwill that he himself was saved from the cruelty of adverse times.[25] No one in this world can be more fortunate than he himself whose desires have been fulfilled after coming under the protection of the emperor.[26] Similar sentiments of the poet can also be noticed in his qasida on Shah Alam II. He compares himself to a seed lying on the barren earth to which only the cloud of the emperor's mercy can give life. Thus, it is only at the threshold of the ruler that unsuccessful men like himself can hope to achieve success.[27]

The success of the monarchical rule is linked by Sauda to certain ideal qualities of the ruler which were regarded as indispensable by medieval writers and thinkers from Abul Fazl to Shah Waliullah.[28] Sauda repeatedly stresses their good qualities such as their sense of justice, generosity, bravery etc. which would compel the powerful to refrain from crushing the weak. No one returns disappointed from the door of his justice and generosity.[29] Sauda writes, 'the emperor's generosity is a catchword among the people which knows no bounds.[30]

In fact it is because of the emperor's kindheartedness and a sense of forgiveness that if people sometimes dare to commit a crime it is because they have faith in his generous and forgiving nature. Otherwise no one dares to violate the laws of the state.[31]

As the success of the medieval kings rested largely on their achievements in the battle field, the valour of the rulers is also emphasized in the qasidas. Sauda extends the eulogization of this quality to their horses, elephants, bows and arrows, swords and shields etc. as the symbols of their military achievements, real or imaginary. The horse of the emperor, for example, is always "as restless as mercury", to embark on fresh conquests. It runs so fast that even the wind in vain seeks to kiss its rein.[32] In other words, nothing but success awaits the kings military adventures. Good fortune follows the emperor, success acting as his *tarqava* (give way) while victory precedes him every where.[33] Even as he mounts his horse, good fortune calls out *Bismillah*.[34]

Such an exaggerated account of the rulers' invincibility by the poet reflects the attitude of society which considered the monarch's cause as the just one, hence deserving victory.

Although Sauda himself favours monarchical rule as the only form of good government, a number of his verses also point towards his consciousness of the weakness of the monarchy during the eighteenth century. The decline of the king's authority and frequent instances of derogation, particularly in case of Jahandar Shah and Farrukhsiyar which invited the ridicule of a poet like Jafar Zatalli, throw light on the failure of the monarchy in fulfilling its social role. Sauda is more cautious in his approach, while refraining from direct criticism of the Mughal monarchy, he points to the dangers inherent in the neglect of its duties towards the subjects. He advises the rulers to avoid any such lapse of responsibility. A ruler should display a correct sense of judgement in appointing his subordinates. He should not employ public officials who manage the affairs of the state to the disadvantage of the people.[35] Similarly in recruiting soldiers he should be able to distinguish between true valour from the mere act of getting one self killed.[36] It would be a pity that a ruler who is considered the deputy of God on earth should be ignorant of the rules which determine the efficiency of the state:

A king is known as God's deputy on earth
How can he fail, but administer justice?[37]

جو شخص نائب داور کہائے عالم میں ٭ یہ کیا ستم ہے نہ آئین داوری جانے

Sauda concludes by pointing out that the true greatness of a monarch depends on his acting on these principles rather than on the mere act of adorning the golden crown.[38] A ruler who fails to adhere to these standards is like a cock who might claim royalty on the basis of its crest:

A ruler who is vainly proud of his crown
Is like a cock with a crest, pretending to be a king of the world.[39]

یہ فخر تاج تو یوں نزد فہم ہے جس طرح ٭ خروس آپ کو سلطان خاوری جانے

It is clear that Sauda's views on the monarchy are not confined to mere eulogization but also high light many of its shortcomings. His persistent and monotonous praise of the emperors like Alamgir II and Shah Alam II, the assigning of identical personal qualities and achievements, the use of hyperbolic similes to describe their so-called pomp and prestige are more in the nature of praising the institution rather than the individual achievements of these rulers. In fact, one might suggest that by drawing an idealized picture of the institution, Sauda is subtly commenting on the lack of these ideal qualities in the rulers of his own day. The poet, it may be assumed found no special achievements which could be attributed to them as he does in the case of praising the administration of Aurangzeb, the victories of Akbar[40] and Shujauddaulah.[41] Sauda, significantly, highlights the achievements of both Akbar and Aurangzeb without any apparent religious prejudice. His qasidas on the emperor, in fact, express a formal allegiance to the Mughal monarchy as the symbol of imperial authority in the eighteenth century. The attitude towards the monarchy did not undergo any change even after Shah Alam accepted Maratha protection in 1784. One of the Maratha sardars praises the emperor in the traditional style of qasida.

> He (Shah Alam) uprooted oppression
> And extended the hand of love and mercy
> when the situation demanded, he could be in rage like Halaku
> He could also be kind and merciful like Jamshed.[42]

غبار ظلم زدو دو کف کرم بکشاد ے بگاہ قہر ہلاکو بمہسرچوں جمشید

The eulogies written on the emperors represent contemporary attitudes towards the Mughal monarchy. In the case of Sauda, he himself was never dependent on the patronage of any emperor as he was well provided for by his own patrons. One of his patrons in Delhi, moreover, was Imadulmulk, the Wazir of Alamgir II, whose relations with Prince Ali Gauhar were strained to the extent of enmity. The Prince fled from the capital, rather than submit to the tyranny of the Wazir[43] and lived in exile till his restoration in 1772. The incident probably provoked Sauda, in view of his close association with Imadulmulk, into writing a short satirical poem on Prince Ali Gauhar, ridiculing his claims to the Wizarat.[44] Sauda, however, later wrote a qasida, welcoming the accession of the prince, in the tradition of the conceptual framework of the ideal of kingship, which he is believed to have presented to Shah Alam when he arrived in Farrukhabad on his way to Delhi in 1771.[45]

Sauda occasionally hints at the rapidly deteriorating position of the monarchy. In one of his verses he refers to the drying up of revenue resources supporting the imperial household,[46] for by the middle of the eighteenth century, the only source of revenue left for the king were the grain markets and salt marts near the capital.[47] The following verse of Sauda highlights the decline of monarchical authority.

> The king no longer heeds the cry of his subjects.[48]

سنتا نہیں ہے درد رعیت کا بادشاہ

Sauda's contemporary poets including Mir wrote few eulogies on the Mughal emperors. Mir's only qasida on the 'contemporary emperor' is monotonous and even half hearted in its objective and barely adheres to the poetic convention of writing a qasida on the reigning king.[49] Other poets like Hatim, Mazhar Jan-i-Janan, Mir Dard and Nazir Akbarabadi did not even fulfil this formality. Hatim lamenting on the decline of monarchical authority writes:

> Spring and autumn has no difference for us,
> For now kings no longer possess a sense of justice.[50]

جہاں کے باغ میں یکساں ہے اب خزاں و بہار ؎ شہوں کے بیچ عدالت کی کچھ نشانی نہیں

Mir who had stayed in Delhi longer than Sauda, gives a detailed account of the pitiable condition of the Mughal emperors Ahmad Shah, Alamgir II and Shah Alam II in his autobiography.[51] He was also witness to the barbarous deed of the blinding of Ahmad Shah (2nd June, 1754) which he mentions with deep sorrow:

> The dust of their feet was once precious collyrium
> I lived to see those very kings cruelly blinded.[52]

شہاں کہ کحل جواہر تھی خاک پا جن کی ؎ انہی کی آنکھوں میں پھرتے سلائیاں دیکھیں

In another verse he comments on the sad plight of the Mughal emperor Shah Alam II, comparing the emperor's poverty with his own destitute condition:

> Friend, you have turned out to be a begger like Shah Alam.[53]

سو تو نکلے ہو کورے بالم تم ؎ ہو گدا جیسے شاہِ عالم تم

The above verse of Mir carries little exaggeration for contemporary accounts relate several incidents which throw light on the poverty stricken state of Shah Alam II. The king on one occasion could not pay the drum beaters a sum of rupees 125 and asked them to be satisfied with a rupee and four annas only. Otherwise it was beyond the capacity of his majesty to pay even such a paltry sum.[54] Indeed, generosity itself required a prosperous age, points out Mir, for how can one expect generosity from any one when the king himself goes hungry.

> It is all very well to be generous and charitable,
> The question is whether the king can afford this?
> When he himself is living, hand to mouth
> And pangs of hunger have reduced him to a skeleton.[55]

دینے کا ہو کہیں ٹھکانا بھی ۓ جود کو چاہئے زمانہ بھی
یاں نہیں گھر میں شہ کے دانا بھی کبھو ہوتا ہے پینا کھانا بھی
ورنہ بھوکے رہے ہیں بیٹھے نڈھال

Even long before Mir and Sauda highlighted the decline of the monarchy, the authority of the Mughal emperors had steadily declined since the days of Jahandar Shah and Farrukhsiyar. The emperor was reduced to the position of a mere shadow under the rule of the Syed brothers who exercised supreme control over the king who even lost his personal liberty to talk to any one without the presence of one of his guardians.[56] Mughal rule at the centre, after the death of Muhammad Shah, had nothing but the name left to it.[57] Ahmad Shah, who succeeded Muhammad Shah had no experience of administration or war and was forced to assign all his functions to the superintendent of the harem, Javed Khan.[58] The next emperor, Alamgir II also remained a puppet in the hands of his all powerful wazir Imadulmulk.[59] In January 1757 some leading Mughal nobles including Abdul Ahmad Khan (third pay master) called the chief sadr and had the Khutba read in the name of Ahmad Shah Abdali while the emperor was alive, and had not been slain, made prisoner or expelled. There is no evidence to show that this had been done at the instance of Abdali, it was on the other hand the work of sycophants who wished to gain favour of the conqueror. Alamgir II could retaliate by merely retiring with his family to the Shah Burj quarter of the palace.[60] The situation was saved by Ahmad Shah Abdali himself who was not interested in occupying the throne of Delhi.[61] The reign of Alamgir was in fact marked by further deterioration of the authority of the king whose efforts to rid himself of his powerful wazir, Imadulmulk only led to the end of his own life. His successor, Shah

Alam II was destined to spend the first twelve years of his reign in exile while the years following his restoration in 1772 only further contributed to the extinction of Mughal political authority in the eighteenth century.

The restoration of Shah Alam II to his ancestral throne may be regarded as a landmark in the history of Mughal sovereignty as the Marathas, who were instrumental to the return of the emperor to the capital, did not go beyond the act of restoration though the empire seemed clearly within their reach. In a couplet written on his way from Agra to Delhi in 1784, the king gives expression to his state of helplessness and dependence on the Maratha sardar, Mahadaji Sindhia.

> Having lost my kingdom and wealth, I am now in your hands
> Do Madho as you like.[62]

ملک و مال سب کھو کر پڑے تمہارے بس ؎ مادھو ایسی کیجو آوے تم کو جس

Similar sentiments of total dependence and resignation to fate are expressed by Shah Alam in a most pathetic elegy written after the loss of his sight at the hands of Ghulam Qadir Rohilla. The emperor appeals to the Marathas, the English and Nawab Asafuddaulah to avenge his insult and restore him to kingly splendour:

> Redress my wrongs and kingly rights restore
> Thee too o Sindhia, illustrious chief
> who once didst promise to afford relief
> Thee I invoke, exert thy generous aid,
> And ye, o faithful pillars of my state
> By friendship bound, and by my power elate
> Hasten, o Asaf and ye English chiefs
> Nor blush to sooth an injured monarch's griefs
> But stay my soul, unworthy rage disown
> Learn to sustain the loss of sight and throne
> Learn that imperial pride and star clad power
> Are but the fleeting pageants of an hour.[63]

The failure of the contending powers to fill the political vacuum when Mughal power lay prostrate was a clear indication that sovereign authority still lay with the Mughal emperor. No attempt was made by any power to replace Shah Alam II who himself, despite his disability and helpless position, remained very particular about his status as the nominal sovereign of India. Notwithstanding the decayed condition of Delhi many independent states repeatedly applied to be received as subjects and tributaries and sought confirmation of all titles and posts from the emperor.[64] The sovereign rights of the Mughal emperors, namely the khutba and the sikka continued to be respected throughout the eighteenth century. Coins of every contending power were struck in his name and the princes of highest rank still continued to display the insignia and titles derived by their ancestors from the Mughal Kings.[65] Moreover no sentence of the criminal court extending punishment of death could be passed without the sanction of the Mughal emperor even after the British occupation of the capital in 1803.[66] Leaving aside an occasional instance of open defiance of the imperial authority, such as the visit of the Sikh leader, Baghel Singh, to Delhi who refused to greet the emperor in the traditional Mughal form with customary words of submission, was allowed to greet the emperor with *Sat Sri Akal*. Even in this case, however, a Mughal chamberlain performed the customary obeisance on behalf of the Sikhs.[67] In the case of the British though the governor general Warren Hastings stopped the payment of the annual tribute, he continued to send formal professions of 'fidelity' and 'attachments'. The British attitude till the close of the 18th century remained one of respect for Mughal dynasty and admiration for Mughal culture which finds expression in the contemporary British writings on India.[68]

The outward show of imperial authority however could not conceal the hard reality that Shah Alam and his successors could only lead the life of a pensioner while the real power gradually passed into the hands of the British. Shah Alam conveyed the bitter truth to his heir apparent, Prince Akbar Shah, in 1802; that the emperor was merely a high class pensioner and his sons should not consider themselves more than that.[69] The emperor overcome by the spirit of resignation and despair reconciled himself to the role of the titular head while leaving all 'good and evil' affairs of the state to the 'will of God'.[70]

Shah Alam, who himself had tried to revive Mughal fortunes in Bihar and Bengal in his youth, was unable to overcome the obstacles which prevented the late descendants of Timur from recovering the extensive dominions and power once enjoyed by their great ancestors. The emperor's strong propensity for ease and indolence described by Polier[71] was not so much a reflection on his character, but it was the decline suffered by the Mughal monarchy which left him with few options in political matters and brought out the fatalist in him:

Just now I have wine and the beloved
Comfort is all mine
When the present is fine
Why bother about the hereafter? [72]

صبح تو جام سے گذرتی ہے ، شب دل آرام سے گذرتی ہے
عاقبت کی خبر خدا جانے ، اب تو آرام سے گذرتی ہے

The long reigns of Muhammad Shah (1719-1748) and Shah Alam II (1759-1806) were not marked by continuous moral decline an aspect wholly ignored by the poets including a satirist like Sauda. Moral decline of the emperors was therefore, not so much personal as institutional, a consequence rather than the cause of the political decline of the Mughals in the eighteenth century.

The fact of the decline of Mughal authority to the extent that revival was impossible was realized by society at large including the litterateurs in the early decades of eighteenth century[73] who finally reconciled to this decline after the sack of Delhi in 1739 and 1757 and readily accepted the patronage offered by local and provincial rulers who had assumed independence on the break down of the central government. The 'Sun of Timoor' was probably set for ever, yet the idea of sovereign authority still remained embodied in the Mughal monarchy for another half a century.

NOTES

1. Mir, *Kulliyat*, Volume I, p. 296.
2. Abu Muhammad Sahr, *Urdu Men Qasida Nigari*, Lucknow 1979, Aqiq Ahmad Siddiqi, *Qasaid-i-Sauda*, Aligrah, 1976.
3. Ziauddin Barani, *Fatwa-i-Jahandari*, Advice IX, translated by Muhammad Habib and A.U.S. Khan, as *The Political Theory of the Delhi Sultanate*, Aligarh, p. 55. Abdul Fazl, *Ain-i-Akbari*, translated by Blochmann, New Delhi, 1965, pp. 1-2. According to Abul Fazl the rulers "take with the assistance of God the burden of this world. A king is, therefore, the origin of stability and possession.... If royalty did not exist the storm of strife would never subside nor selfish ambition disappear".
4. Sauda, *Kulliyat*, I, pp. 158-159.
5. *Ibid.*, pp. 160-161.
6. *Ibid.*, II, p. 262.

7. Many contemporary accounts substantiate this point. More than two decades after Mir and Sauda's departure from Delhi, Shah Alam II in spite of old age and blindness continued to command respect as the nominal sovereign of India. W. Franklin, *Asiatic Researches*, Vol. IV, pp. 427-228; Twining, *Travels in India a hundred years ago*, pp. 234-235. Palmer to Hastings, 29th October, 1789, B.M. ADD, quoted, P. Spear, *Twilight of the Mughals*, p. 29.

8. Ziauddin Barani, *Fatwa-i-Jahandari*, p. 55; Abul Fazl, *Ain*, pp.1-2.

9. Savitri Chandra Shobha, *Social Life and Concepts in Medieval Hindi Bhakti Poetry*, New Delhi, 1983, pp. 76-77; Harbans Mukhia, 'Aspects of State and Society: As Reflected in Dadu Dayal's Granthaval, *Proceedings of Indian History Congress*, Chandigarh, 1973.

10. Sauda, *Kulliyat*, II, p. 100.

11. *Ibid.*, p. 160.

12. *Ibid.*

13. Satish Chandra, (edited) R.E. Frykenberg, *op. cit.*, p. 212.

14. Sauda, *Kulliyat*, I, p. 158.

15. *Ibid.*, II, p. 152.

16. *Ibid.*, I, pp. 159-160.

17. K.M. Ashraf, *Life and Conditions of the People of Hindustan*, New Delhi, 1970, pp. 68-69.

18. Abul Fazl, *Ain*, I, Blochmann, pp. 52-54.

19. Sauda, *Kulliyat*, II, p. 100.

20. *Ibid.*, I, p. 159.

21. *Ibid.*

22. *Ibid.*, p. 160.

23. *Ibid.*

24. *Ibid.*, II, p. 100.

25. *Ibid.*, I, p. 159.

26. *Ibid.*

27. *Ibid.*, p. 160.

28. Abul Fazl, *Ain*, pp. 3-4; Shah Waliullah, *Hujjatullah Baligha*, Urdu translation, Abdul Haq Haqqam, Karachi, Volume I, pp. 92-94.

29. Sauda, *Kulliyat*, I, p. 159.

30. *Ibid.*

31. *Ibid.*

32. *Ibid.*, p. 160-161.

33. *Ibid.*, p. 161.

34. *Ibid.*, p. 159.

35. *Ibid.*, II, p. 100.

36. *Ibid.*

37. *Ibid.*

38. *Ibid.*

39. *Ibid.*, p. 101.

40. *Ibid.*, I, p. 169.

41. *Ibid.*, pp. 182-184.

42. Firaqi, *Waqa-i-Alamshahi*, pp. 67-68.

43. Ghulam Husain, *Siyarul Mutakherin*, Translation (Urdu) Gokul Prashad, Lucknow, 1874, Volume III, pp. 59-60; Anonymous, *Tarikh-i-Alamgir Sani*, British Museum MS, 108, b, Ali Gauhar had been appointed Wazir by Ahmad Shah Abdali on 19th February 1757 but later due to the intrigues of Imadulmulk the post was given to him by Abdali, quoted, J.N. Sarkar, *Fall of the Mughal Empire*, Volume II, p. 112.

44. Sauda, *Kulliyat*, II, p. 173.

45. A.A. Siddiqi, *op. cit.*, pp. 16-17.

46. Sauda, II, p. 263.

47. *Delhi Chronicle*, quoted, Sarkar, II, p.4.

48. Sauda, II, p. 226.

49. Mir Taqi Mir, *Kulliyat*, II, pp. 18-22, Abu Muhammad Sahr, *op. cit.*, p. 101.

50. Zahuruddin Hatim, *Diwan-i-qadim*, (ed.) Abdul Haq, Delhi, 1977, p. 205.

51. Mir, *Mir Ki Ap Biti*, pp. 109, 118-119, 190.

52. Mir, *Kulliyat*, I, p. 133.

53. Mir, *Kulliyat*, II, p. 109.

54. Firaqi, *Waqa-i-Alam Shahi*, p. 97.

55. Mir, *Kulliyat*, II, p. 426.

56. Khafi Khan, *Muntakhab ul Lubab*, 816, 831; Muhammad Ali Khan, *Tarikh-i-Muzaffari*, MS. Azad, 218, 224.

57. Ghulam Husain, *Siyar*, III, p. 25.

58. *Tarikh-i-Ahmad Shahi*, 136-15a; quoted J.N. Sarkar, *Fall of the Mughal Empire*, Volume I, pp. 205-206.

59. *Tarikh-i-Alamgir Sani*, 4b-5a; *Tarikh-i-Muzaffari*, p. 98, quoted J.N. Sarkar, *Fall of the Mughal Empire*, Volume II, pp. 2-3.

60. *Tarikh-i-Alamgir Sani* 93b-95b, quoted J.N. Sarkar, *Fall of the Mughal Empire*, Volume II, p. 67.

61. *Ibid.*

62. Firaqi, *Waqa-i-Alamshahi*, p. 67.

63. W. Franklin, *The History of the Reign of Shah Aulam*, pp. 257-258.

64. A.L.H. Polier, *Shah Alam and his Court: A Narrative of the Transactions at the court of Delhi from the year 1771*. Edited by P.C. Gupta, Calcutta, 1947, pp. 41-42; W. Hamilton, *Description of Hindostan*, Reprint, Delhi, 1971, Volume I, p. 422.

65. W. Hamilton, *Description of Hindostan*, p. 422.

66. *Ibid.*, p. 417.

67. H.R. Gupta, *History of the Sikhs*, Delhi, 1980, Volume III, pp.169-170.

68. Alexander Dow, *History of Hindostan*, London, 1770, Volume II, Jonathan Scott, *History of the Deccan*, Shrewsbury, 1794, Volume II, pp. 305-306.

69. Tekchand, *Roznamcha-i-Shah Alam*, Ms. Khuda Baksh Library, Patna, F. 124, ff.448-49a, quoted in S.A.A. Rizvi, *Shah Abdul Aziz, Puritanism, Sectarian Polemics and Jihad*, Canberra, 1982, p. 43.

70. Firaqi, *Waqa-i-Alam Shahi*, pp. 85-86.

71. A.L.H. Polier, *Shah Alam and his court, A narrative of the Transactions at the court of Delhi from the year 1771*, pp. 67-69.

72. Firaqi, *Waqa-i-Alam Shahi*, p. 72.

73. Jafar Zatalli, *Kulliyat-i-Jafar Zatalli*, (ed.), Naim Ahmad, Aligarh, 1979.

4

THE NOBILITY

Kings are ruined and in disgrace the nobles fare no better
Perhaps what they need is the society of a recluse.[1]

خراب و خوار ہے سلطاں شکستہ حال امیر ؎ کسو فقیر سے شاید کہ صحبت ان کو نہیں

The nobility formed an indispensable organ of the monarchical system, sharing with the king the social responsibility of acting as the protector and caretaker of the welfare of the people. The decline of the authority of the Mughal emperor since the early years of the eighteenth century, left a deep impact on the character and role of the Mughal nobles who responded to the new political situation by carving out their own independent islands of power. The poets who saw the decline of the central authority with the initial sense of shock and dismay were gradually reconciled to the political realities by pinning their hope and faith in the establishment of stability, law and order by capable men, both from within the nobility as well as the aspiring new adventurers who appeared on the political scene in the eighteenth century.

Nobles and Politics

The poets attach great significance to the political role and functions of the nobility. They do not refer to its composition or struggle within its ranks for the leading offices of the empire which had begun after the death of Aurangzeb.[2] But they do highlight the economic disparities among the nobles, their changing loyalties, intrigues and corruption as the contributory factors in the decline of the imperial government. The poets at the same time also lay great stress on the traditional role of the nobles in which certain personal ideal qualities, such as, valour, loyalty, benevolence, sense of justice and patronage of men of letters are considered to be of utmost importance in the proper functioning of the state.[3] In this context Sauda praises the ideal qualities of his patron, Imadulmulk, who had been appointed Wazir of the empire.

> Have you not heard, Ghaziuddin Imadulmulk, previously Mir Bakshi
> Is now the wazir of an empire, considered to be a model of the kingdom of heaven.[4]

سنا نہیں ہے کہ غازی دیں عماد الملک ؎ جو میر بخشی تھا واں کا اب ہوا ہے وزیر

Sauda elaborates on the personal qualities and administrative ability mostly imaginary, of Imadulmulk in highly exaggerated tones. To him, under Imadulmulk's guidance, the administration of Aurangzeb's times, based on Islamic principles seems to have been resurrected "a miracle no less amazing than that of Christ".[5] Sauda's praise of Imadulmulk's administration is far removed from reality in view of the breakdown of the central administration and preoccupation of the wazir himself in military affairs, to give serious attention to matters of administration. His reference to the Islamic nature of Aurangzeb's administration and its revival under Imadulmulk's guidance is again questionable. Sauda's reference, how ever may seem to be significant in the light of the efforts made by the emperor Alamgir II, to follow in the footsteps of his great ancestor, Alamgir I.[6]

Sauda's eulogization of Imadulmulk, therefore, though seemingly removed from historical reality, does throw light on the attitude of the poet who betrays the contemporary tendency to look back to the past glories of the Mughals to seek inspiration in the predominantly unstable political conditions at the centre. It is interesting to note that in spite of the poet's close proximity to the wazir, he does not mention the weakness of his position during his wizarat of five and a half years.

This tendency to gloss over the failures and to focus attention on the real and supposed achievements of the members of the ruling class is quite apparent in his other qasidas written in praise of Nawab Shujauddaulah,[7] Nawab Asafuddaulah,[8] Saifuddaulah,[9] Basant Khan, Sarfarazuddaulah[10] and others. The nature of eulogization of these nobles is universally monotonous, Sauda for instance, does not see any difference in the military capabilities of Imadulmulk or Shujauddaulah on the one hand and of Sarfarazuddaulah and Saifuddaulah on the other. Mir betrays a similar attitude in his qasidas written on the emperor[11] or the nobles.[12]

The subject of the decline of the empire, which attracted the attention of all the poets, is seen chiefly in terms of the decline of the nobility. Sauda, for example, discusses at length, the role of the nobles vis-a-vis the decline of the empire. He notes with regret that the loyalty of the nobles so vital for the proper functioning of the state is absent as most of them concentrate on acts of self aggrandizement. On the one hand, as a warning to them, Sauda satirizes the nobles who show laxity in their loyalty towards the state and on the other, reminds them of their duties and responsibilities.[13]

Sauda considers the leading nobles of the empire engaged in constant internal strife to have been responsible for the debacle of the imperial forces (at Karnal) and the subsequent and repeated ravaging of the capital at the hands of the invaders. In an obvious reference to the court politics and factional fights that followed the defeat at Karnal and the departure of Nizamulmulk from the capital who had secured for himself, the post of Mir Bakshi, Sauda writes:

High and low ranking officials discuss affairs of state
As they parley and intend to act
The Mir Bakshi thinks of retiring to his own Subah
While the wazir casts greedy eyes on the silver coverings of the royal tent.[14]

جو مصلحت کے لئے جمع ہوں صغیر و کبیر ؎ تو ملک و مال کا فکر اس طرح کریں ہیں مشیر
وطن پہنچنے کی سوجھی ہے بخشی کو تدبیر کھڑا یہ اٹکلے دیوان خاص بیچ وزیر
کہ شامیانہ کے بانسوں پہ نقرئی ہیں پھول

Condemning the disloyalty of the nobles and their indifference to the fate of the empire, Sauda exclaims that if they have any shame left they should "bury themselves alive".[15]

Mir, similarly finds most nobles at the court, corrupt and disloyal:

Those having even a slight influence in court circles
Are cheats, tricksters and traitors, indulging in malpractices.[16]

ہے جنہیں کچھ بھی رویتِ دربار ؎ سو فریبندہ و مسکری و غدّار

Sauda's long *Shahr Ashob*, written in 1757, refers to the plight of Alamgir II's government in 1756-1757 when Delhi was threatened by the appearance of Ahmad Shah Abdali's forces in the north. The government found itself totally demoralized and incapable of preparing for the defence of the empire. The wazir, Imadulmulk refused to march to Sirhind to oppose the invader as he had no money to raise an army. He however, wrote letters summoning the Marathas and the Jat Rajah but they too demanded money.[17] The greatmen of the city of Delhi meanwhile made preparations for flight, most of them sending their families to Agra and Mathura under the jurisdiction of Suraj Mal. The family of Raja Jugal Kishore,[18] a patron of Mir, left Delhi for Mathura while the emperor and the wazir, powerless to fight, sent piteous appeals to Abdali to spare Delhi.[19] An important section of the nobility, points out Sauda, had thus lost its old vigour and sense of responsibility:

> The nobles do not know the art of making war or peace
> While the wise among them have deserted them.[20]

نہ رسم صلح کی سمجھیں نہ جنگ کا دستور ۔ جو ان میں قاعدہ داں تھے ہوئے وہ آن کے دور

Sauda's *Shahr Ashob* thus substantiates contemporary reality as the capital was left totally defenceless, an act for which the wazir, Imadulmulk, was reprimanded by no other person than the invader himself.[21]

A few capable officers who still remained in the capital, points out Sauda, confine themselves to the security of their houses, spending most of their time in the company of their friends and flatterers.[22] They dislike entertaining any visitors, and if at all they agree to see a person, they refuse to discuss the affairs of the state, saying "Brother, for Gods' sake speak of something else".[23] The nobles of the age, to Mir were not merely indifferent to political affairs but were most corrupt, to the extent that only the most corrupt ones could gain access to them:

> Four bad characters act as their servants
> And with ten soldiers they claim to hold a durbar.[24]

چار لچّے ہیں مستعدِ کار ؛ دس تلنگے جو ہوں تو ہے دربار

In another verse, Mir satirically points out:

O Mir, do not meet the contemporary nobles,
For we have been ruined because of their wealth.[25]

نہ مل میرؔ اب کے امیروں سے تو ؎ ہوئے ہیں فقیران کی دولت سے ہم

What emerges from contemporary poetry is the political indifference of the ruling class towards the fate of the empire rather than a decline of character and morals of the nobility. The eulogization of the nobles who had virtually assumed independence may be noted in this context. The praise showered by Sauda and Mir on those nobles who had succeeded in establishing themselves as virtually independent rulers reveals an interesting dichotomy in the attitude of the literati towards the empire and the ruling classes. Both Mir and Sauda although sharply critical of the nobles who seemed no longer keen on the revival of the empire, lamenting at their 'selfishness' and indifference, do not hesitate to eulogize Shujauddaulah and Asafuddaulah[26] who established themselves as de facto independent rulers in Awadh. The eulogization of their personal qualities, wealth, and grandeur and their devotion for the welfare of their subjects,[27] implies that the literati who had taken shelter in Awadh and other independent kingdoms, were prepared to accept those rulers who had successfully assumed the responsibility of establishing peace, law and order in which arts could flourish in their respective states. Besides, they also saw a possibility of continuance of Mughal ideals of government and cultural traditions under their rule.

The following verse of Sauda expressed the contentment and prosperity of Asafuddaulah's state, which stands in contrast to the chaotic state of affairs in the capital described by the poet himself in the *Shahr Ashob*:

Peoples' contentment and prosperity in your reign defies description
If a passerby sees a pearl lying on the way side
He kicks it away with indifference
Never has gold been treated with such disdain.[28]

جو گدا روز و شب کہ سائل تھا ؎ چاہئے رشکِ خسرواں ہووے
در و دروازہ یوں ہے اب کس کا ؎ کہ نہ واں پیل و پیلباں ہووے

At another place in the same qasida Sauda relates the prosperity of the subjects of the Nawab with great hyperbole:

Those who once begged for food, day and night
Are now so prosperous
That even kings should envy them
Is there any house today
That does not have an elephant or a Mahavat at its door.[29]

خلق کو اس قدر ہے استغنا ؏ نہیں ممکن کہ وہ بیاں ہووے
رہرو آگے پڑا ہو گوہر ؏ دور ٹھوکر سے گر رواں ہووے

Again, to Mir, who himself had experienced extreme poverty and had been a witness to the misery and bankruptcy of the Mughal emperors in Delhi, the age of Asafuddaulah seemed to fulfil the ideal of good government and opulence:

O cup bearer look! A royal party is on
But be all attention. The great Asaf is there in person
Let us join it with a cup in hand and a bottle under the arm
Renowned as he is for his generosity and benevolence
He may honour us with conferment of the Khilat.[30]

منعقد مجلسِ شہانہ ہے ؏ ادبِ آصفِ زمانہ ہے

آ کہ ساقی مجھے قرابہ دے ؏ در بغل شیشہ ساتھ اپنے لے

بحرِ بخشش کی لہریں اب آئیں ؏ زر و گوہر کی کشتیاں لائیں

ہے بلند اس کرم کا کیا پایہ ؏ دیتے ہیں خلعتِ گراں مایہ

In case of Sauda, he does not confine himself to the mere eulogization of the provincial rulers but also advises them to keep a watch on the elements of instability and disorder such as heretics, atheists and hypocrites in the kingdom.[31] His analysis of the potential enemies of the state however is essentially limited nor does he elaborate or find necessary linkages in the process that contributed to the weakness of the state during his times. His verses, however do reflect his anxiety regarding the state's defence against all possible forces of disharmony and disintegration. The righteousness of the rulers cause is also emphasized by Sauda in his praise of the nawabs of Awadh. Thus in the long poem on the victory of Shujauddaulah over the Rohilla chief Hafiz Rahmat Khan,[32] Sauda credits his patron with victory not merely on the ground of personal bravery or the help of the English, but mainly because of the righteousness of the ruler's cause. His praise for Asafuddaulah's position as the wazir of the empire[33] really signifies the growing power of the provincial kingdoms vis-a-vis the central government as the office of the wizarat had been reduced to a mere shadow of its original authority by this time.

In the eulogization of the provincial nobility, Sauda does not hesitate from including the comparatively new entrants in the bureaucracy. In a number of short poems, he showers praise on Sarfarazuddaulah Hasan Raza Khan[34] who had risen into importance during the reign of Asafud-daulah. He had served as an ordinary durban (door keeper) under Shujauddaulah and had participated in the battle of Miran Katra fought against Hafiz Rahmat Khan, along with Shujauddaulah as *Darogha-i-Top Khana*.[35] He was appointed Naib in the reign of Asafuddaulah on the advice of the British resident. Sauda also wrote a qasida on Richard Johnson, who was the Naib of the resident of Lucknow, Nathanial Middleton, under the title of Mumtazuddaulah Hasan Jung Richard Johnson.[36]

Sauda or Mir do not attempt to establish any causal link between the powerful position of their patrons who had assumed independence with the weakness of the central government. Objectively seen, to the poets, a section of the nobility which succeeded in establishing political and economic stability in their respective states deserved to be praised and their authority accepted regardless of the fate of the Mughal empire.

Nobles and Economy

The *Shahr Ashobs* of Sauda and Mir along with those composed by their older contemporaries like Shakir Naji and Hatim not only highlight the economic plight of the nobles in Delhi but also substantiate other sources in evaluating the nature of the economic crisis and its repercussions on the lives of the people, from the noble man to the soldier and from the poet to the merchant and traders.

The economic crises depicted by the poets chiefly relates to the decline of the imperial capital and need not, therefore, be generalized to reflect the economic condition of the nobles living outside the imperial territories. Sauda and Mir who themselves speak of the poverty of the nobles of Delhi also relate the grandeur and affluence of the ruling classes in Awadh[37] where the two poets spent the last years of their lives.

Delhi, however, remained the focal point of the poet's attention as it experienced its worst political and economic crises in the years 1739 to 1760. Shakir Naji who was in the army of Muhammad Shah which was routed at Karnal wrote a long *Shahr Ashob*[38] on the impact of the military defeat on the government as well as on society in general. Hatim, who wrote the *Shahr Ashob*, a few years before the great debacle, noted the plight of the nobles in view of the bankruptcy of the central government which further deteriorated after 1739.

Descendants of the great nobles
Once at the height of affluence, face poverty
Yet are too vain and astounded
To reconcile to changed conditions[39]

امیر زادے ہیں حیران اپنے حال کے بیچ ؎ تھے آفتاب پر اب آگئے زوال کے بیچ
پھرے ہیں چرخ سے ہر دن تلاشِ مال کے بیچ ؎ وہی گھمنڈ امارت ہے پھر خیال کے بیچ

Again, Hatim points to the pathetic condition of the majority of the nobles in Delhi:

Nobles are reduced to the status of grass cutters
Those who once resided in Palaces
Do not possess even ruined houses to give them shelter[40]

جہاں میں صاحبِ خسخانہ گھاس والے ہیں ؎ جنھوں کے محل تھے ان کو کھنڈر کے لالے ہیں

Mir who himself suffered extreme hardships voices the same sentiment.

> What is to be gained by lamenting the fate of the poor, like Mir
> Here many great men, have been reduced to dust.[41]

تو ہے بیچارہ گدا میر ترا کیا مذکور ؎ مل گئے خاک میں یاں صاحب افسر کتنے

Sauda, not merely highlights the economic crisis of the nobility, but also discusses the possible reasons for its decline. He attributes the crisis to the drying up of their sources of income. Referring to the crisis of the jagirdari system, he correctly points out that no money reaches the nobles from their jagirs, consequently resulting in their inability to maintain the required number of contingents.[42] The condition of the department dealing with the assignment of jagirs, namely, *daftar-i-Tan*, is such that orders regarding the issue of jagirs have lost all value. Even a grocer would not hesitate in tearing up an order for the issue of a jagir, to wrap his goods.[43] As no revenues reach the treasury from the Khalisa or jagir lands, it results in the bankruptcy of the state. In such a situation every one, from the soldier to the mutasaddi remain without employment.[44] Sauda also laments the desperate condition of both the naqdi and jagir holding mansabdars who are unable to find any work:

> All the mansabdars holding cash or jagir assignments
> Are equally helpless in finding a source of income.[45]

یہ جتنے نقدی و جاگیر کے تھے منصب دار ؎ تلاش کر کے ڈھلتے انھوں نے ہو ناچار

These nobles are forced to live on credit after giving away even their sword and shield to the local money-lender and when even this source is exhausted they are left with no alternative but to take to begging in the streets.[46]

Sauda comes very near contemporary reality when he points out that the crisis of the mansabdari system was not confined to the holders of small ranks but extended to those holding high ranks as well.[47] The problem of the ever increasing number of jagirdars, highlighted by Bhimsen[48] in the last decade of the seventeenth century, further deteriorated under the successors of Aurangzeb due to lavish grant of jagirs. A large number of people were given high ranks between 6000 to 7000 with titles of Jang, Malik, Rai and Raja during the reign of Bahadur Shah with the result that mansabs lost their significance.[49] According to Sauda, one should not assume that if one managed to secure a mansab of seven thousand he would be relieved of all his troubles. He mentions the name of one Mansur Ali Khan, who in spite of holding the rank of seven thousand was unable to live comfortably.[50]

The evidence summarized above reflects Sauda's remarkable understanding of the financial crisis of the nobles, as he refers to it not in isolation but against the breakdown of the mansab-jagir system. Sauda's lament at the failure of the government in receiving revenues from the Khalisa or jagirs lands points to the misappropriation of the imperial revenues by a handful of powerful nobles[51] causing great misery to the majority of the nobles who were left without jagirs. Sauda's assertion that "nothing is realized from the rabi or Kharif"[52] highlights the plight of these jagirless nobles as well as of the imperial government which found itself bankrupt at the end of Muhammad Shah's reign. It was a time, Nazir wrote, when the prosperity of the recent past seemed to have been snatched away as if by the cruel blow of death, taking with it the great men of the age.

> Time was when Amir Khan and Khan-i-Khanan were big names
> Death pounced upon them with a tiger like paw,
> Leaving none on the scene nobles, richmen and All.[53]

کہتا تھا کوئی دیکھو یہ ہیں امیر خاں جی ؎ اور یہ ہیں خانِ خاناں اور یہ ہیں میر خاں جی
پنجہ اٹھا قضا کا جب آکے شیر خاں جی ؎ پھر کس کے میر خاں جی کس کے وزیر خاں جی

Mir repeatedly laments the utter destitution of a large number of nobles, who unable to draw their salaries faced starvation. Thus:

> Those who were once proud rulers
> Today do not even get alms in Delhi.[54]

دلّی میں آج بھیک بھی ملتی نہیں انھیں ؎ تھا کل تلک دماغ جنہیں تاج و تخت کا

Or

> Mir, what to speak of the nobles of this age
> They are all destitutes and beggers.[55]

کیا کہئے اپنے عہد میں جتنے امیر تھے ؎ ٹکڑے پہ جان دیتے تھے سارے فقیر تھے

Mir Dard, who lived a life detached from worldly affairs, also occasionally comments on the declining fortunes of the nobles:

> Men who once led a life of luxury, are without means of livelihood.
> They are like a sparkling spring that has gone dry.[56]

بے بضاعت ہیں سب اہلِ زرق و برق ؛ چشمہ خورشید میں کدھر ہے آب

Dard shares with his fellow poets, a regret at the decline of the nobles of Delhi.

> Adversity has turned the affluent into labourers
> This pains Dard deeply.[57]

مے کشاں کرنے لگے محنت کشی ؛ درد ہوتا ہے دلِ یاراں کباب

The economic decline of a large section of the nobility in the imperial territories thus remains a subject of great distress for the poets. It also implied a breakdown of the patronage system resulting in large scale unemployment and hardships for professional groups.

Sauda and Mir who highlight the economic plight of the nobles in Delhi repeatedly refer to the problem of unemployment in the capital along with its social and economic implications. Mir looks at the problems characteristically in the light of his own experience.

> I have to wander about even for a handful of salt
> And get grievously hurt for its sake.[58]

مشتِ نمک کی خاطر اِس واسطے ہوں حیراں ؛ کل زخم دل نہایت دل کو مرے لگا تھا

How long could Mir burden himself with the worries of livelihood? Only, death would release him of these worries. In more specific terms, he writes:

> Now thousands of people are without employment
> Only a few lucky ones succeed in getting some work.[59]

اب سب کے روزگار کی صورت بگڑ گئی ؛ لاکھوں میں ایک دو کا کہیں کچھ بناؤ ہے

Hatim who lived in Delhi and saw the decline of the city before his eyes, takes shelter in the ideal of contentment:

> O Hatim do not regret at the revolution of times
> For you are not lacking in bread or employment.[60]

تو انقلاب زمانے میں غم نہ کھا حاتم ؎ کہ تجھ کوں رزق بہت اور روزگار ہزار

In an other verse he points to the problem of unemployment directly.

> God provides daily bread to all his creatures
> And yet I see many without bread.[61]

عالم کی ہے گی رزقِ الٰہی سے زندگی ؎ تس پر بھی دیکھتا ہو بہتوں کو ناں نہیں

The problem of unemployment is highlighted in one of the *Shahr Ashobs*[62] of Sauda at great length. In the context of the problem of unemployment Sauda discusses various possibilities of finding employment but rejects each of them because of the inability of the nobles to provide the people, from the soldier to the poet, with work. A person might get himself enrolled in a noble's army but it is doubtful whether he would ever be successful in collecting his salary, at least not in his life time, that is, it is bound to fall into arrears which was a common occurrence during the 18th century.

In such a situation, points out Sauda, the soldiers rarely remained in possession of both his shield and the sword for either of these is usually pawned for paying for the fodder for his horse.[63] In these circumstances the soldier is thus forced to live on the mercy of the money-lender otherwise his wife and children go hungry for days together.[64] It is only after repeated threats and warnings that the soldiers manage to wrest from the nobles their pay for two months although the arrears run for thirty six months.[65] In fact the whole reign of Alamgir II had been marked by the unrest and rowdiness among the soldiers because of non-payment of their salaries due to the financial bankruptcy of the central government. On 10 August, 1754, when even half a month's salary was not paid on the 19th, the imperial diwan, Nagar Mal was stoned by the emperors' servants.[66] Such incidents were also witnessed in the earlier reigns. Shakir Khan, a court historian of Ahmad Shah's reign described the financial bankruptcy at the accession of the new emperor. According to him the descriptive list of all articles in the imperial stores, including carpets, arms, cooking pots, utensils and books was prepared and these articles were sold to the shopkeepers and pedlars. Most of the money realized was spent in paying the troops who remained dissatisfied and forcibly carried away valuables and articles from the houses of wazirs, amirs, traders and shopkeepers and sold them to realize their own arrears.[67]

Mir joins Sauda in elaborating on the weakness of the imperial forces in the following verse:

In the army, wherever one may glance
The soldiers are hungry and desperate.[68]

فوج میں جس کو دیکھو سو ہے اداس ؎ بھوک سے عقل گم نہیں ہیں حواس

The demoralization of the soldiers, the pitiable condition of the animals of the army such as horses and elephants described by Mir[69] and Sauda,[70] complete the picture of the destruction of the imperial armies. Sauda elaborates on the weakness of the Mughal armies, in a number of verses including his satire, *darhajv Asp Tazhik-i-Rozgar*,[71] which was written in the last years of Muhmmad Shah's reign. The satire, ostensibly on an impoverished noble and his horse was really a commentary on the breakdown and demoralization of the imperial forces which were hardly in a position to face an adversary in the field of battle. Sauda himself seems to have witnessed the rout of the imperial armies:

When I (Sauda) came face to face with the Maratha
The horse refused to move out of sheer weakness
And when I saw the issue of the battle decided
I ran for my life, with shoes in my hand
And horse under my arm.[72]

یہ کہہ کے میں خدا سے ہوا مستعد بجنگ ؎ اتنے میں مرہٹہ بھی ہوا مجھ سے آدو چار
گھوڑا تھا بسکہ لاغر و لیست و ضعیف و خشک ؎ کرتا تھا یوں خفیف مجھے وقت کار زار
جب دیکھا میں کہ جنگ کی اب یاں بندھی ہے شکل ؎ لے جوتیوں کو ہاتھ میں گھوڑا بغل میں مار

The significant point that emerges from Sauda's amusing hyperbole is the breakdown of the imperial armies in Delhi by the middle of the eighteenth century. Hence the idea of finding employment in the imperial army seemed futile to Sauda.

The profession of the soldier, however, remained a popular one in other parts of India during the same period. A large number of people continued to enroll themselves in the armies of the provincial rulers or the zamindar levies. Besides the regular soldiers, a large number of people were recruited as camp followers, accompanying each army. In 1782, for example, 20,000 troops of the Nawab of Awadh on his campaigns were accompanied by a further, 1,50,000 camp followers.[73] Thus a large number of people, in spite of the breakdown of the mansabdari system, continued to depend for livelihood on the expenditure of the armies and even draw reasonably high salaries. A gentleman trooper drew as much as Rs. 100 per month and on ordinary trooper Rs. 15 as monthly stipend in Awadh.[74]

Along with the profession of a soldier, the plight of other similar groups mentioned by Sauda should be examined chiefly in the context of the problem of unemployment in Delhi and its surrounding areas. Sauda found the profession of a *musahib* or a close companion to the noble no more profitable than that of a soldier. His life would become intolerable in trying to adjust even his sleep and hunger according to his whims.[75] One could also become a physician to a great noble for a hundred or two hundred rupees but the noble's continuous harassment would make the life of the physician unbearable. Even if he sneezed, the physician would be called to diagnose its cause.[76] To find employment as wakil to a nobleman,[77] according to Sauda, would be an equally frustrating experience in view of the declining fortunes of the nobility. The wakil makes the pretence of representing his noble's interests at the capital regarding his application for the grant of jagir. His time is spent in paying visits to the various offices, including that of the Diwan, Bakshi and the Bayutat, trying desperately to convince each department of the capabilities of his master.[78] He succeeds in duping the *muwakkil* (agent) of the money-lender and disappears with the money advanced by him. Finally he hides in the house in fear of being caught for the duplicity. But if the agent happens to come his way he tries to convince him that he has been able to get words, 'sanction' or granted on the application and 'issued' on the *Siyaha.* All this manoeuvring on the part of the wakil, points out Sauda, really shows his struggle to save himself and his family from starvation otherwise.

> Everything concerning an application.
> A *siyaha, parwana* or jagir

Had long lost all significance.[79]

کاہے غرض عرضی اور کس کا سیاہا ؎ کیدھر کا وہ پروانہ وہ جاگیر کہاں ہے

The profession of a poet,[80] points out Sauda, fares no better, for no one is such a prey to worries as the poet who has to keep a constant watch on the pockets of his potential patrons. When at last he finds a "suitable" patron, his whole attention is directed towards pleasing him by all means possible. Sauda's reference to the plight of his own profession highlights the misery of a large number of poets who were forced to leave Delhi in search of patrons. Mir for example repeatedly speaks of his extreme misery due to lack of patronage in the capital.

Do not lament at my miserable condition
This is the result of the vicissitudes of times.[81]

میرے تغیر حال پہ مت جا ؎ اتفاقات ہیں زمانے کے

The condition of the *Khatibs*, (preachers) and *katibs* (calligraphers) was equally bad for they seem to be no longer hired for their services. Writing on the miserable condition of the *Katibs*, Sauda points out that no one asks for the service of these clerks, not even at the rate of hundred pages, for a dime.[82] They sit idle on the road sides, or at the most they may be hired to write a book or a sale deed for just a dime or so. Even the Shaikhs have been reduced to great poverty and the only hope left to them is to make appeals to some noble or the other to save their wives and children from starvation.[83]

Sauda also discusses the difficulties of the merchants who brought costly luxury goods to be sold to the nobles. But laments the poet, goods brought from such far flung places like Isfahan find no market in Delhi and the merchants have to travel as far as Deccan to sell their articles.[84] If some noble agrees to buy these goods, its payment is rarely made, and he even he accuses the merchants for selling stolen goods, and on this pretext fixes a very low price.[85] However, even then the payment is evaded, sending the merchant on a wild goose chase to collect his dues first from the noble's amil, who in turn reveals the utter bankruptcy of his master advising the merchant to collect his goods from the *diwan-i-bayutat*, as he was not in a position to pay the dues on behalf of his master. But the goods are not traceable, the merchant in the end loses his goods as well as his money.[86]

Sauda's account of the plight of the merchants engaged in trade in luxury goods in Delhi signifies the bankruptcy of the nobles who were forced to cut down their expenditure and consumption in view of the repeated looting of Delhi and neighbouring territories in the mid-eighteenth century. It also highlights the disruption of trade on the old imperial trade routes passing through the cities of Lahore, Agra and Delhi.[87] The decline of the old trading centres like Delhi or Agra, however, did not imply an overall decline of trade and credit relations in northern India.[88]

Finally not only the professional groups enumerated above, who seemed to have been dependent on the nobles' patronage but other destitute and unemployed people also looked upon the nobles for providing them with a source of livelihood. Sauda describes a number of idle men who roam about in the streets or just sit out side the shops and whenever a nobles' procession passes, they run towards it to relate their grievances. If the noble does not oblige them, they follow his carriage, crying aloud as if they were following a funeral procession.[89]

The foregoing analysis shows that the poets' attention was primarily drawn towards the declining fortunes of the ruling class in a period of great desolation and ruin of Delhi brought about by the constant movement of invading armies of Nadir Shah, Ahmad Shah, Marathas, Jats, Afghans and Sikhs. The decline of the nobles in the capital certainly implied unemployment and hardships for a large section of the population as economic life was closely linked with the fortunes of the empire and its ruling classes. Despite the preoccupation of the poets in enumerating chiefly the miseries of the urban population in the light of the decline of the patronage system there are passing references on the rural scene and on the plight of the cultivators. Sauda, for instance in one of his *shahr Ashobs* highlights the difficulties of the peasants in the rural areas around Delhi where constant movement of armies had virtually destroyed cultivation:

> If a farmer is lucky enough
> He possesses land and a pair of bullocks
> If rains are also favourable
> He is a happy man
> Otherwise he lives in constant fear of drought and attachment

Deprived of peace of mind and comfort of the heart.[90]

دو بیل کی بہا کرو جو کہیں کیجیے کھیتی ؎ اور مینہ بھی موافق ہے پڑے تو توسماں ہے
ہیں خشکی و قرقی کے تفکّر میں شب و روز ؎ نہ امن ہے دل کے تئیں نہ جی کو اماں ہے

Economic life suffered a heavy set back in the years Sauda and Mir lived in Delhi though economic activity did not cease altogether in the city.[91]

The following verse of Nazir more than captures the attitude of the poets and of their society towards the passing away of the old Mughal nobility from active economic life of the cities of Delhi and Agra:

There once lived celebreties called Nawabs and Khans
If one was known as son of a panch hazari
The other was held in high esteem for noble descent
And possessed great wealth, jagir and mansabs
Yet, they have all vanished suddenly leaving no trace behind.[92]

کتنے دنوں یہ غل تھا نواب ہیں یہ خاں ہیں ؎ یہ ابنِ پنج ہزاری یہ عالی خانداں ہیں
جاگیر و مال و منصب گو آج ان کے ہاں ہیں ؎ دیکھا تو اک گھڑی میں نہ نام و نہ نشاں ہیں

Nobles and Society

The impoverishment of a large section of nobles in Delhi was a serious set back to their social standing, style of living, values as well as relations with other sections of society. The declining fortunes of the nobility and its inability to fulfil its social obligations became a matter of deep regret as well as censure in the poetry of Hatim, Mir and Dard. In the case of Sauda his approach is both satirical and sermonizing. But beneath these tones of apparent exaggeration and literary rhetoric, there is a vivid and powerful narration as well as a critical review of the social evils which the poet considered to have crept into the leading sections of society.

The poets woefully note that the nobles who once lived in grandeur are now faced with starvation with the result that many of them have been forced to sell their luxurious articles in order to survive. Hatim notes with regret that,

Strange seem the nobles of today
without fear of God, without spiritual guidance
Fate makes them move in circles
Like the revolving sun and moon.
Such is the plight of the enlightened ones.[93]

عجب احوال دیکھا اس زمانے کے امیروں کا ؛ نہ ان کو ڈر خدا کا اور نہ ان کو خوف پیروں کا
مثالِ مہر و مہ دن رات کھاتے چرخ پھرتے ہیں ؛ فلک کے ہاتھ سے یہ حال ہے روشن ضمیروں کا

In this hour of trial Hatim advises the nobles to take to the path of contentment.

Let men of low birth be proud of wealth and riches.
For men of noble birth take pride in wealth of poverty.[94]

تو کیا ہوا کہ رجالے کے زر سیتی پت ہے ؛ ہے افتخار نجیبوں کا فقر و دولت عار

Mir and Sauda adopt a more critical attitude towards the declining fortunes of the nobles and their failure in fulfilling their social obligations. To Mir the cause of their decline is not so important as their indifference and pride which to him, is the chief cause of his own miseries:

Do not meet the nobles of the age
It is their wealth that has made us poor.[95]

نہ مل میر اب ان امیروں سے تو ؛ ہوئے ہیں فقیر ان کی دولت سے ہم

Sauda, in a number of poems satires, describes the plight of the nobles, who despite their strained circumstances still wish to cling to their old paraphernalia of dignity. It is no longer possible for most of them to afford grand processions with *piyadas* (foot soldiers) preceding and mounted soldiers, following them.[96] The trumpet, the flywhisk and the fur cloak seem to be the only remaining symbols proclaiming their hollow dignity and prestige. Even their women, traditionally confined to strict confinement, have come out of their houses in ordinary burqas. They stand in the streets carrying in their arms their lovely babies, but as they are too ashamed to beg, they offer for sale, rosaries made from the holy clay of karbala.[97] If the condition of the nobles continued to decline like this laments Sauda, then it would not be long when most of them would be reduced to utter poverty.

The critical financial condition, of a sizable section of the nobility, as highlighted by Sauda, affected their relations with other social groups, their value system and above all the proverbial generosity and hospitality expected of a nobleman of the age. Sauda at length, laments at the decline of the old values, the violation of etiquette as well as their lack of benevolence and graciousness. To him, it was the abandonment of these features by the nobles which caused decay in their social standards. In this context Sauda lampoons a rich nobleman for ignoring the most valued standards of behaviour expected of a nobleman.

Ostensibly the satire is focused on a nobleman's miserly behaviour towards an unexpected guest but in reality it is a critical commentary on the changed values and patterns of living, Sauda noticed in the society of his day. The poet begins the satire by relating an incident of how one of his friends happened to visit a rich nobleman and the treatment meted out to him in his house.[98] The great noble instead of welcoming the guest soon became obsessed with the idea of getting ride of him as heavy clouds had started gathering and he did not wish his guest to spend the night at his house. When it started to rain, he became even more agitated. Ignoring all rules of courtesy, he repeatedly asked his servant to see whether the clouds had cleared and even brought out a rain coat to make his guest leave the house.[99] In his naivete the guest did not take the hint and declared his intention of spending the night at the noble's house as he believed, considering the status of his host, that he could be easily provided for a night's stay.[100] On hearing this, the noble was even more alarmed and with a sigh enquired.

> My friend, why did it rain so much
> That the question of (your) spending the night came up.[101]

کیوں بھلا ابر اس قدر چھایا ؛ حرف رہنے کا درمیاں آیا

After cursing his bad luck as well as the rain which continued to pour down till late at night, the host at last excused himself on the pretext of visiting the toilet, asking his guest to order what he pleased for dinner.[102] The steward who appeared only after repeated callings told the guest that no food could be served as the provisions had been exhausted. He pointed out that even the local *bania* refused to supply provisions to the nobles because of non-payment of grocery bills.[103] Similarly, the butcher often threatened the nobles' cook with his knives while the vegetable seller insulted him by agreeing to sell to him only the cheapest available vegetables such as the pumpkin.[104] Even the local *kababi* and bread seller, further pointed out the steward, refused to have any dealings with the noble as they did not receive a dime for their goods.[105]

An analysis of this long satire shows that the nobles lack of hospitality or lack of manners can not be attributed to his sheer miserly nature which Sauda emphasizes. What is objectively reflected in the satire is the nobles' embarrassing financial condition which is the cause of his reluctance to entertain a guest even on a small scale. Sauda's reference to the nobles' mounting credit to the local tradesmen throws more light on his bankruptcy rather than his miserly behaviour. This is clear from the poet's account of the nobles establishment. Even the kitchen reflects the nobles poverty. No rich food is ever prepared; the cooks invariably suffer from running noses while water carriers run towards the kitchen if they see smoke rising from its chimneys thinking the house to be on fire.[106]

Sauda's satire, shorn of its apparent exaggeration and humour, really points to the difficulty of a section of the nobles in maintaining the old standard of extravagant living. It is in this context that the nobles' anger at his son's desire to entertain a friend even at a frugal level has to be studied. Therefore, the simplest gesture of hospitality by the son like offering lentils and bread to the guest is looked upon with dismay by the noble.

> There is nothing left, like hoarded wealth any more
> All that is left is to sell the bricks of this house[107]

گڑے پیسے یہ سب اڑا دے گا ؎ اینٹوں تک بیچ بیچ کھا دے گا

The satire on the 'miserly noble', therefore, need not be dismissed as merely another example of Sauda's craftsmanship in this form of poetry. Its chief target is not the individual noble but the contemporary nobility which in a state of bankruptcy could not fulfil its social obligations and the consequent laxity that had crept in their social behaviour. This is clear from the fact that Sauda has not attributed the satire to any particular individual which was a common practice in his times.[108] Besides the economic plight of the miserly nobleman' described in the satire can be well corroborated to similar conditions related by the poet in his other verses.[109]

The impact of the failure of the nobles in the performance of their social duties and obligations, can be further noticed in Sauda's other satires which throw light on the changing relations of the bankrupt nobles with their dependents and servants. In these verses the picture of the traditional position of the nobles commanding unquestionable awe and respect from their servants and from those lower in status, is singularly absent. Instead, it is marked by an absence of all fear and respect as well as an attitude of open isolence and defiance towards the master in view of the inability of the nobility to maintain its huge establishments by the middle of the eighteenth century, a process which had begun in the last decades of the seventeenth century.[110]

Sauda gives several instances of the dissatisfaction of the nobles' servants. In most cases this attitude was the result of the non-payment of their salaries by the noble concerned which had resulted in near starving condition of the noble's servants.[111] According to Sauda, they curse their fate lamenting on the futility of an employment when "even eating a single chapati requires such desperate attempts". In another case a servant complains that even if he managed to receive his dues, these are inadequate for survival; adding with a sigh.

> God knows if ever I received more than eight annas
> I do not know whether the rupee is made round or flat in this age.[112]

وہ نوکر اب جسے آقا ہر آن پہچانے ؛ جو پوچھو اس سے کہ تم کچھ روپے لگے پانے
کہے ہے آہ وہ بھر کر سوائے آٹھ آنے ؛ روپے کی شکل نہیں دیکھی ہے خدا جانے
کہ اس زمانے میں چپٹا بنے ہے وہ یا گول

The servant responsible of laying the noble's table, for instance, abuses the master's taste "which is expensive though his stomach is invariably empty". Similarly, the other servants of the noble including the cook bitterly curse the master for not paying them their salaries.

In such circumstances, points out Sauda in his *Shehr Ashob*, the servants of the nobles refuse to heed their commands. The master might order his cook to prepare *pulao* but he instead abuses him and prepares nothing better than broth. Or if a noble asks his *farrash* to straighten the carpet, he would not hesitate from pulling away the *masnad* itself from under the noble.[113] Similar behaviour of the servants is portrayed by Sauda in an other Satire.[114] The cause of open defiance in this case being the master's worsening financial condition which had resulted in non-payment of their salaries.

Sauda begins the satire by relating an incident when the relations of a noble and his servant reached a breaking point because of the former's wish that the latter should prepare a dish of crow.[115] As the meat remained raw, the master accused the cook for having drunk the ghee while preparing the dish. The cook retorted at the allegation that he would not even touch it as the crow to him was as unlawful and dirty as pork. When the master hit him in great anger, he did not hesitate in returning the blows, and the servants prepared for a battle:

> The onlookers tried pacifying the noble, exclaiming,
> How dare these miscreants misbehave with the master.[116]

لوگ ان کو تھامتے تھے یہ کہتے تھے ہے غضب ؎ آقا کو مجھ سے یوں کہے یہ ابلہ بے ادب

After a prolonged fight the servants of the noble demanded that they should be paid their arrears of salary as they were tired of having to live on just a handful of grains.[117] The nobles' feeble threat to continue the fight failed as he had not a dime to pay his servants, hence in great helplessness agreed to make peace with them.[118]

The above satire of Sauda brings out the nature of relationship between an impoverished noble and his numerous servants. The open defiance on the part of the servants points to the loosening of the bonds of subordination, yet they do not leave their master since there was little scope for finding employment elsewhere in the capital. Sauda himself, though satirizing the nobles, does not approve of the servants rebellious and insolent attitude towards the master, condemning their behaviour as outrageous, Sauda declares at the end of the satire.

> The rascals were eventually successful
> And the master had to tolerate them in spite of insolence.[119]

القصّہ کتنی دیر رہی جب یہ بات چیت ؎ ہارے میاں نفرے ہوئی پاجیوں کی جیت

Hatim joins Sauda in his lament at the decline of the nobles' once honourable position in society.

> O Hatim, this age favours the rascal and the mean
> The noble and the honest have fallen on bad days.[120]

حاتم اب وقت ہے رجالوں کا ؁ خوار و خستہ پھرے ہیں جگ میں نجیب

NOTES

1. Mir, *Kulliyat*, I, p. 492.
2. For details see Satish Chandra, *Parties and Politics at the Mughal Court*, pp. 242-257; Z. Malik, *The Reign of Muhummad Shah*, pp. 182-188.
3. Sauda, *Kulliyat*, I, pp. 168-169; 173-174, 176-177, 186-187; Mir, *Kulliyat*, II, pp. 14-15, 16-17.
4. Sauda, *Kulliyat*, I, pp. 167-168.
5. *Ibid.*, p. 169.
6. *Tarikh-i-Alamgir Sani*, 4b-5a, *Tarikh-i-Muzaffari*, p. 98, quoted, J.N. Sarkar, *Fall of the Mughal Empire*, Volume II, p. 2.
7. Sauda, *Kulliyat*, I, pp. 172-184.
8. *Ibid.*, pp. 184-193.
9. *Ibid.*, pp. 201-212.
10. *Ibid.*, pp. 212-218.
11. Mir, *Kulliyat*, II, pp. 18-22.
12. *Ibid.*, pp. 13-17.
13. Sauda, *Kulliyat*, II, pp. 262-263.
14. *Ibid.*, p. 263.
15. *Ibid.*
16. Mir, *Kulliyat*, II, p. 420.
17. *Tarikh-i-Alamgir Sani*, 85a-86a, quoted, J.N. Sarkar, *Fall of the Mughal Empire*, Volume II, p. 60.
18. Mir, *Mir Ki Ap Biti*, p. 129.
19. *Delhi Chronicle*, *Tarikh-i-Alamgir Sani*, 90b, quoted, J.N. Sarkar, *Fall of the Mughal Empire*, Volume II, p. 61.
20. Sauda, *Kulliyat*, II, p. 262.
21. W. Irvine, 'Ahmad Shah Abdali and the Indian Wazir Imadulmulk', *Indian Antiquary*, p. 44.
22. Sauda, *Kulliyat*, II, p. 262.
23. *Ibid.*
24. Mir, *Kulliyat*, II, p. 419.
25. *Ibid.*, I, p. 350.
26. Sauda, *Kulliyat*, I, pp. 176-177, 186-187, 193; II, p. 165; Mir, *Kulliyat*, II, pp. 14-18, 186-187, 201-202.

27. Sauda, *Kulliyat*, II, pp. 174-176, praises the building activity of Asafuddaulah, including the construction of wells and mosques.

28. *Ibid.*, I, pp. 184-185.

29. *Ibid.*, p. 185.

30. Mir, *Kulliyat*, II, pp. 166-167.

31. Sauda, *Kulliyat*, I, p. 174.

32. *Ibid.*, pp. 182-184.

33. *Ibid.*, p. 193.

34. *Ibid.*, II, pp. 170-171; II, pp. 196-201; A.A. Siddiqi, *op. cit.*, pp. 22-23.

35. Najmul Ghani, *Tarikh-i-Awadh*, II, p. 157.

36. Sauda, *Kulliyat*, I, (ed.) Muhmmad Hasan, Delhi, 1969, p. 36.

37. Mir, *Kulliyat*, II, pp. 158-159, 166-167, 186-187; Sauda, *Kulliyat*, I, pp. 184-185.

38. Mohammad Husain Azad, *Ab-i-Hayat*, p. 105.

39. Hatim, *Diwan-i-Qadim*, p. 274.

40. *Ibid.*, p. 275.

41. Mir, *Kulliyat*. I, p. 225.

42. Sauda, *Kulliyat*, II, p. 262.

43. *Ibid.*, p. 263.

44. *Ibid.*

45. *Ibid.*

46. *Ibid.*

47. *Ibid.*

48. Bhimsen, *Nuskha-i-Dilkusha*, English translation in *J.N. Sarkar Birth Centenary Commemoration Volume*, (ed.), V.G. Khobrekar, Bombay, 1972, pp.166, 231-232.

49. Khafi Khan, II, pp. 628, 629, 630; *Siyar*, II, pp. 6-7.

50. Sauda, *Kulliyat*, I, p. 230.

51. *Tarikh-i-Ahmad Shah*, 14b, 20b, 21a; Tarikh, Shakir Khan, MS. B.M., p.35, quoted J.N. Sarkar, *Fall of the Mughal Empire*, I, p. 215; *Tarikh-i-Alamgir Sani*, 22, 28-29, quoted J.N. Sarkar, *Fall of the Mughal Empire*, II, p. 24.

52. Sauda, *Kulliyat*, II, p. 262.

53. Nazir Akbarabadi, *Kulliyat*, p. 160.

54. Mir, *Kulliyat*, I, p. 54.

55. *Ibid.*, p. 712.

56. Mir Dard, *Diwan-i-Dard*, p. 36.

57. *Ibid.*

58. Mir, *Kulliyat*, I, p. 69.

59. *Ibid.*, p. 231.

60. Hatim, *Diwan-i-Qadim*, p. 208.

61. Hatim, *Diwanzada*, in *Shah Hatim, Halat Aur Kalam*, (ed.) Ghulam Husain Zulfiqar, Lahore, 1964, p. 309.

62. Sauda, *Kulliyat*, I, pp. 226-230.

63. Sauda, *Kulliyat*, I, p. 226.

64. *Ibid.*

65. *Ibid.*

66. *Tarikh-i-Alamgir Sani*, 8a, 12b, 13b, 18a, 22b, 26, 32a, 29b-30a, 37b-79a, *Delhi Chronicle*, quoted J.N. Sarkar, *Fall of the Mughal Empire*, Volume II, p. 19.

67. Shakir Khan, *op. cit.*, p. 34, quoted J.N. Sarkar, *Fall of the Mughal Empire*, Volume I, pp. 216-217.

68. Mir, *Kulliyat*, II, p. 415.

69. *Ibid.*, p. 419.

70. Sauda, *Kulliyat*, II, p. 262.
71. *Ibid.*, I, pp. 230-234.
72. *Ibid.*, p. 234; also, Mir, *Kulliyat*, II, pp. 210, 418-419.
73. William Tenant, *Indian Recreations consisting chiefly of strictures on the Domestic and Rural economy of the Muhammadans and Hindoos*, London, 1802, Vol. II, pp. 356-366.
74. W. Irvine, 'The Bangash Nawabs of Farrukhabad' *Journal of Asiatic Society of Bengal*, XLVII, part I, 1878, p. 264.
75. Sauda, *Kulliyat*, I, p. 227.
76. *Ibid.*
77. *Ibid.*
78. *Ibid.*, 228.
79. *Ibid.*, *Siyaha* (Statement of Accounts) *Parwana*, (a royal order under seal).
80. *Ibid.*, p. 229.
81. Mir, *Kulliyat*, I, p. 243, also, p. 353.
82. Sauda, *Kulliyat*, I, p. 229.
83. *Ibid.*, pp. 229-30.
84. *Ibid.*, p. 227.
85. *Ibid.*, p. 228.
86. *Ibid.*
87. A. Das Gupta, 'Trade and Politics in the eighteenth century India' in D.S. Richards, (ed.), *Islam and Trade of Asia*, Pennsylvania, 1970, p. 195.
88. *Ibid.*, pp. 183-84.
89. Sauda, *Kulliyat*, I, pp. 226-227.
90. *Ibid.*, p. 228.
91. Husain, *Murtaza*, *Hadiqatul Aqalim*, pp. 44-45. Forster, *op. cit.*, pp.141, 191, 218; W. Frankin, *Asiatic Researches*, IV, p. 424.
92. Nazir, *Kulliyat*, p. 160.
93. Hatim, *Diwanzada*, p. 119.
94. Hatim, *Diwan-i-qadim*, p. 208.
95. Mir, *Kulliyat*, I, p. 350.
96. Sauda, *Kulliyat*, II, p. 262.
97. *Ibid.*, p. 266.
98. *Ibid.*, I, pp. 289-295.
99. *Ibid.*, pp. 289-90.
100. *Ibid.*, p. 190.
101. *Ibid.*
102. *Ibid.*, p. 291.
103. *Ibid.*
104. *Ibid.*
105. *Ibid.*, p. 292.
106. *Ibid.*, p. 294.
107. *Ibid.*
108. Sauda, *Kulliyat*, II, p. 194-199, satire on Mir Zahik, for example, has a personal bais.
109. Sauda, *Kulliyat*, I, pp. 226-230, II, pp. 261-266.
110. Athar Ali, *The Mughal Nobility under Aurangzeb*, Bombay, 1970, pp.161-169.
111. Sauda, *Kulliyat*, II, p. 265.
112. *Ibid.*
113. *Ibid.*, p. 264.

114. *Ibid.*, pp. 257-260.
115. *Ibid.*, p. 257.
116. *Ibid.*, p. 258.
117. *Ibid.*, p. 259.
118. *Ibid.*
119. *Ibid.*, p. 260.
120. Hatim, *Diwan-i-qadim*, p. 108.

5

MYSTICISM, SYNCRETISM AND ISLAM

Our Search for God in Kaaba or Temple
Proved Futile
Where shall we find him now? Any guidance.[1]

حرم و دیر تو ہم چھان چکے ، کہیں اس کا بھی نشاں پائیے گا

The Mughal Legacy

The eighteenth century religious scene, contrary to the generalisation regarding the "decline and stagnation" of religious life during this period was not barren of creative activity and even proved to be a fertile one in terms of religious literature. The diversity of religious beliefs and practices intermingled to give an eclectic and tolerant atmosphere to an age which was marked by experiments and reforms in different parts of the country. The beginnings of reforms may be noticed in regions where Christianity or western influences had not penetrated. Thus, significantly growing independently of foreign impact.

A large number of renowned scholars and reformers emerged whose aim was to free religious life of its corrupt practices and arouse it from its state of ritualism and superstition. Most of the Hindu reformist sects which sprang up in mid-eighteenth century worked for the spiritual and moral upliftment of the masses, especially the lower strata of society, recognising no caste or communal barriers. The satyanami sect in U.P. founded by Dulandas, a Rajput of Kotawah, the sect of Sivnarayan founded in 1734 by another Rajput of Sesana; the Balrami sect founded by Balram Hari and the sect of Katra Bhajas founded by Aulechand, worked for the upliftment of the down trodden in Hindu society.[2] Another outstanding Hindu reformer, Prannath, founder of Pranami Sampradaya, in his work entitled *Kulzum Sarup*, tried to show that there was great similarity in the philosophy embodied in the Vedas and the Quran.[3] A common feature of these sects was belief in monotheism, condemnation of ritualism and caste system and an encouragement to the ideals of religious tolerance and humanism. The following comments of a contemporary foreign observer highlight the growing popularity of the reformist sects:

> "Indeed of late years, sectarianism has spread in India, particularly among the once orthodox Hindus not a few of whom are passing from gross idolatory into the abstract non-entities of 'deism'". He further hoped that soon this would prepare the way for the spread of Christianity in india.[4]

The Muslim religious outlook shared a striking similarity with its Hindu counterpart. In Bengal, for instance, Muslim writers of mystical literature made free use of indigenous terms and concepts to underline the difference between scriptural and mystical positions. The Shariat, for examples representing the esoterical and formal aspects of Islam was identified with Hindu Sastra or scripture.[5] By the end of the eighteenth century and early nineteenth century many Islamic themes came to be recast in the Hindu mould while many Hindus wrote in praise of the Muslim Pirs.[6] The challenge from the forces of orthodoxy spearheaded by the movement of Shaikh Ahmad Sirhindi (1653-1724) during the early seventeenth century seemed to have been tided over in the writings of liberal scholars and sufis like Mian Mir (1550-1635) Shaikh Muhibullah (1587-1648), Dara Shikoh (d. 1658) and Sarmad (6d. 1660). Although orthodox teachings remained dominant at the imperial court in Aurangabad.[7] Delhi remained the centre of liberal mystical tradition of the time of Jahanara and Dara Shikoh, richly contributing to the strengthening of the eclectic outlook of the eighteenth century which may be noticed in the revival of the Chishti order by Shah Kalimullah (1650-1729). These tendencies received further encouragement by the adoption of liberal and conciliatory policies by Bahadur Shah I[8] and his successors. The attempt of Nizamulmulk to return to orthodox policies including a suggestion to reimpose Jazia met with opposition from a large section of the nobles.[9] The experiment in orthodoxy and the reimposition of Jazia, had already failed during the seventeenth century demonstrating the practical impossibility of basing the state in India on Shariat and of making a distinction between Hindus and Muslims.[10] The orthodox policies associated with Aurangzeb, therefore, had to be given up within a decade of his death.

Political conflicts notwithstanding Hindu-Muslim relations remained cordial, with mutual respect for each other's faith. Many Hindu chiefs including the Marathas continued to venerate Muslim sufi saints, Mahadaji Sindhia and his son Daulat Rao were followers of Mansur Shah. Mahadaji is said to have pledged an offering at the tomb of Mansur for his victories over Ghulam Qadir, Ismail Beg and the Rajput Rajas.[11] The Marathas at the height of their power in Delhi even allowed the slaughter of cows in the capital.[12] The rulers of Bengal and Awadh followed a liberal religious policy. The Nawabs of Awadh offered grants to Vaishnavite priests and Gosains of Mathura and Ayodhya.[13] Asafuddaulah offered patronage to the monotheistic Hindu reformer, Jagjivandas of Kotah, founder of the Satnami sect. In the Punjab Mughal governors like Zakriya Khan continued the imperial tradition of giving land grants to ascetics so that "they may remain occupied with praying for an ever lasting dominion".[14] . . . The Sikh rulers of the province also continued the Mughal policy by confirming earlier grants to the mahants of Pindori.[15]

Several instances of religious conflict during the eighteenth century such as riots in Ahmedabad (1713) on the issue of cow slaughter,[16] riots in Punjab,[17] Delhi (1729), Agra (1720) and Kashmir[18] over conversion to Islam, Holi and Muharram festivals, occasionally marred Hindu-Muslim relations. These instances of communal conflict, however, can be easily over emphasised[19] unless viewed from the larger perspective of Islamic presence and process of Islamisation in India.

In the history of Islamic tradition in India, elements of heterodoxy and orthodoxy confronted each other since the twelfth century onwards in a bid to gain ascendancy as in the reigns of Akbar and Aurangzeb. Although liberal trends remained in ascendancy for most of the period, at the intellectual level confrontation between the two was ever present. Thus, Islamic theological and philosophical precepts and principles existed along with local syncretistic elements as Islam was unable to conquer indigenous religious traditions and their total displacement could be achieved only at the cost of Islam's own rejection. Hence, the sultans and the ruling classes in early medieval period generally refrained from using force in matters of religion and remained contented with consolidation of their political power and social domination.[20] During the 18th century, movements such as that of Shah Waliullah and his successors represent the efforts of the conservative elements to resist the challenge from syncretistic tendencies dominant in the age. Shah Waliullah as the *Qaimul Zaman*,[21] the spokeman philosopher, leader and guide of the age, besides advocating the purification of the religious life of the Muslims[22] also recommended several injunctions against the non-Muslims and Shias.[23] The cry of the orthodoxy, however, remained isolated and unheeded, both at the political as well as the religious level, for it did not result in the repudiation of an overwhelmingly syncretistic culture of the eighteenth century. Even Shah Waliullah's son and successor, Shah Abdul Aziz displayed a liberal attitude towards the Hindus by identifying them with the Muslim philosophers' group (*falasfia*). Various incarnations of God in Hinduism were considered by him as divine symbols whether found in the form of human beings, animals or fishes.[24]

The eighteenth century was the age of the Sufi and the poet who seemed to enjoy larger followings than the theologians whose influence remained largely confined to scholarly circles. The growing syncretistic spirit found literary expression in the rapidly expanding vernacular literature of the period. A large number of these writers wrote in what has been aptly termed as the "mystico-syncretistic" tradition.[25] In Delhi Urdu poetry was not only symptomatic of the prevailing liberal spirit but it also served as an effective vehicle for giving expression to the potential universality of religious thought during this period.

Mysticism

Religion in its simple and popular form seemed to fulfil the requirements of the age. The mystic ideals of trust in God (*tawakkul*), abstinence (*wara*), renunciation (*zuhud*), poverty (*faqr*) and patience (*sabr*) along with the idea that suffering is the precondition of the spiritual bliss and that divine grace would reach those who suffer in patience in order to reach eternal bliss, gained great popularity among the elite as well as the common people. The writings of Mirza Mazhar Jan-i-janan and Mir Dard reveal the true spirit of the eighteenth century mysticism further reinforced by the mystical elements in the Urdu Poetry of the age:

> O God lift the curtain of separation
> that hangs between us,

We are caught in the trap
Give us strength to free ourselves of
worldly allurements.[26]

خداوندا اٹھالے ہجر کے درمیاں سوں پرکے ؎ ہمیں صیاد کے اب دام میں ڈالا ہمیں پردے

These mystical ideals, rather than the age old doctrinal dispute between the followers of *Wahdatul Wujud* and *Wahdatush Shuhud* which Shah Waliullah had unsuccessfully tried to resolve by emphasising the principle of *ijtehad* (speculative reconstruction), held great attraction for the sufi and the poet alike. Although Mirza Mazhar Jan-i-janan, the great Naqshbandi saint of the period, was critical of Shah Waliullah's attempt of reconciling the two doctrines, the Naqshbandi thought during this period was subjected to a much wider and liberal interpretation instead of confining itself to the ideal of "everything is from Him". Perfect sufis, according to Mir Dard, made no distinction between *Wujud* and *Shuhud* though the call of *hamaust* (everything is He) had misled a large number of sufis as well as common people into mere sensuality without reaching the mystical experience.[27]

The leading Chishti saints of the period, especially Shah Fakhruddin of Delhi adopted a conciliatory approach to the doctrinal issue centering around *Wahdatul Wujud* and *Wahdat Ush Shuhud*. Shah Fakharuddin (1714-1785) though himself a strong adherent of Wujud considered disputes about *hamaust* and *hamaazust* as meaningless for nothing besides God existed, who had no beginning or end.[28] Both the Naqshbandi and the Chishti saints were against extreme puritanism in religious matters. Shah Fakharuddin for instance saw no *shirk* (polytheism) in the illumination of graves on the ground that Mecca and Medina were illuminated. Mirza Jan-i-janan[29] and Mir Dard, contrary to the tradition of the Naqshbandis adopted a liberal attitude to *Sama*. The latter continued to hold sama gatherings despite the disapproval of many colleagues, in the tradition of his father, Muhammad Nasir, on every second and twenty sixth day of each month. *Sama* gatherings were also arranged by Shah Abdul Aziz at his uncle's house for Shah Fakharuddin.[30] The sufi saints rebelled against the commercialisation of mysticism by the 'worldly' ones who tended to exploit people for personal gains and whose Khanqahs had lost much of their piety turning them into virtual vice dens.[31] Condemnation of such corrupt practices find ample expression in Urdu poetry of the age. Yet despite the prevailing corruption in Sufi practices[32] of the period under study, the intellectual and organisational vitality generated by various sufi orders cannot be ignored. Its most significant achievement being its popularity as it became acceptable to a larger number of people rather than remaining confined to the Muslim elites.

Mysticism in its varied forms thus became the focal point in the religious life of the Muslims also attracting large sections of the non-Muslim population.[33] The Urdu ghazal of the period is full of mystical expressions centering around the concept of *Wahdatul Wujud* and *Wahdat Ush Shuhud*. The best reflection of the *Shuhudi* concept is noticeable in the poetry of Mir Dard written in the mystical tradition of the Naqshbandis. In several verses, Mir Dard using his favourite image, that of a mirror, fits it into his interpretation of divine transcendence. If the world is regarded as a mirror that reflects God's beauty then it is clear that the mirror and the reflected beauty are two different things.[34] The mirror becomes valuable only by its capacity of reflecting true beauty, thus emphasising the *Naqshbandi* formula of "everything is from Him".

All this multitude will vanish in a
moment
If we look into the mirror and utter
Hoo (God)[35]

مٹ جائیں ایک آن میں کثرت نمائیاں ؎ ہم آئینے کے سامنے جب آ کے ہُو کریں

In another verse Mir Dard gives expression to the state *Khalwat dar Anjuman* that is, solitude in a crowd that marks the end of a mystical experience, a state of perfect tranquility, yet the sufi communicates with the people while his heart at all times remains with God.

The present life is a journey to the
other world
While the eyes look for spectacles, the
heart seeks him.[36]

ہستی ہے سفرِ عدم وطن ہے ؎ دل خلوت و چشم انجمن ہے

Mirza Mazhar Jan-i-janan also wrote in the mystical tradition of the Naqshbandis although he was not a prolific writer of the Urdu ghazal. Mirza Jan-i-janan wrote poetry mostly in Persian but a few of his Urdu verses reflect the concept of *Shuhud*:

> I saw the beauty of the dazzling morning sun in
> its glory
> What I saw was the manifestation of Gods presence
> in all its splendour.[37]

سحر اس حسن کے خورشید کوں جاکر جگا دیکھ ؛ ظہورِ حق کوں دیکھا خوب دیکھا یا ضیا دیکھا

In view of the contribution made by leading Naqshbandi saints, scholars and poets in the development of mysticism in the eighteenth century, the significance of the *Shuhudi* doctrines can hardly be overemphasised. Yet the extent of its impact on the religious life is difficult to evaluate in the light of the growing popularity of the *Wujudiya* doctrine in the last decades of the 18th century.[38] Moreover, as the poets frequently wrote on both the concepts, it is hardly possible to judge the popularity of *Wujud* and *Shuhud* on the basis of their verses. Even in the case of Mir Dard, expression of subjectivism in the tradition of the *Wujudiya* are found in several of his verses:

> O Dard it is beyond my power to resist
> the force of love
> just as dry straw is too feeble to
> resist amber.[39]

اے درد! چھوٹتا ہی نہیں مجھ کو جذبِ عشق ؛ کچھ کہربا سے چل نہ سکے برگ کاہ کا

In a few verses Dard even uses the imagery of intoxication generally used by the Wujudiya for describing the state of ecstasy.

> In My prolonged search for Him, I have
> lost my ownself
> So much so that I now forget in whose search
> I had set off.[40]

اے درد! رفتہ رفتہ کیا آپ کو بھی گم ؛ اس راہ میں چلا تھا میں کس کے سراغ کو

What is more important to note, however, is the expression of common mystical themes by the poets which included the ideals of spiritualism, divine love, relations of man with God, contentment, mutability of human existence, its joys and sorrows etc. which combined to reveal the true spirit of mysticism, leaving a deep impact on contemporary religious attitudes.

The idea of divine love and relations of man with God is a recurring theme in the ghazal. The chief goal for the mystic, according to Mir Dard, is not the union with Him, as for the "intoxicated" ones but forgiveness and at the most, the vision of eternal beauty.

> O Dard, clear the mirror of your heart of impurities
> The Universe will then manifest itself in all its beauty.[41]

اے درد! کر ٹک آئینۂ دل کو صاف   پھر ہر طرف نظارۂ حسن و جمال کر

Man is considered a reflection or manifestation of divine attributes and the highest goal of man is the contemplation of Divine light. This attitude differs from the pantheistic view of an all embracing unity which Dard considered dangerous for the fabric of Islamic religious life. In many verses he appeals to God to lift a veil that covers His traces and grant him a seeing eye which discovers His beauty in the creation.

> The veil of ignorance stood between the beloved
> and ourselves
> That veil gone, He stood revealed (in all His grandeur)[42]

حجاب رخ یار تھے آپ ہی ہم   کھلی آنکھ جب کوئی پردا نہ دیکھا

The *Wujudiya* ideal of regarding the relations of man with God, that is, God and his creation are but two aspects of the same reality, find ample expression in the poetry of Mir, Sauda and Hatim. Mir though not attached to any sufi order expresses the relationship of man with God in the *Wujudiya* tradition.

> I wandered around in quest of God
> Not knowing that realisation of self
> means union with him[43]

تھا وہ تو رشکِ حورِ بہشتی ہمیں میں میر   سمجھے نہ ہم تو فہم کا اپنے قصور تھا

All sublimation and veneration of God is really for oneself. God sent the man to this world to show His manifestation but very few understand this reality.[44]

Our eyes longed to get a glimpse of Him,
But as the curtain rose, we found ourselves
face to face with ourselves.[45]

کب سے نظر لگی تھی دروازۂ حرم سے ؎ پردہ اٹھا تو لڑیاں آنکھیں ہماری ہم سے

Expressing regret at the execution of Mansur Hallaj[46] the famous sufi of Baghdad, Mir writes that had Mansur exercised self-restraint he would not have lost his life, for what he said was too manifest to be denied by anyone.[47] Hatim like Mir expresses his belief in concept of *Wahdatul Wujud* by pointing out that man cannot be seen as a separate entity from God:

Although man is not God
But in reality separated from God
man ceases to exist.[48]

بندہ اگر جہاں میں بجائے خدا نہیں ؎ لیکن نظر کرو تو خدا سے جدا نہیں

Sauda, as in the case of Mir and Hatim, did not follow any particular order of sufis but accepted the basic ideals of mysticism.

We turned to the temple and the Kaaba
in search of God
What a folly! Not Knowing
that this place is in our heart.[49]

دیر و حرم کو دیکھا اللہ رے فضولی ؎ یہ کیا ضرور تھا جب دل کا مکاں بتایا

Asceticism or the idea of darveshi, an essential aspect of mysticism gained great popularity during the period marked by social and political turmoil. The idea of darveshi not only inspired sainthood but also formulated a philosophy of life: the concept of the impermanence of life and the futility of existence inspired sainthood both among the Hindus and the Muslims thus assuming the role of a great unifying factor in the religious attitudes of the people. All the poets from Mir Dard to Mir and Hatim extol the virtues of asceticism. Dard, himself a sufi, praises the path chosen by a darvesh. He is one who does not bear anyone's obligation just as the cypress does not bend its branches with the weight of the fruits.[50]

> All kingdom and riches are dust before
> the fortune of asceticism
> For us *huma* is no better than a crow.[51]

دولتِ فقر کے حضور گرد ہے جاہ و سلطنت ؛ کہتے ہیں یاں جسے ہما اپنی نظر میں زاغ ہے

Hatim who himself had opted for the life of an ascetic in the *Khanqah* of his Pir, Shah Taslim, writes:

> A darvesh does not seek favours from anyone
> Continued deep affliction is his sustenance.[52]

نظر کسی کی یہ نعمت اوپر نہیں رکھتے ؛ ہمیشہ خونِ جگر ہے غذائے درویشاں

A true qalandar is one, writes Mir, who remains in constant ecstasy, leaving aside intellect as his guide.[53] If one wishes to opt for such a life he must sacrifice his faith as well as worldly goods, honour and dignity.[54] Sauda though more realistic and down to earth, also extols the path of asceticism.

> Sauda those who chose the path of darveshi
> Remain unaffected by the ups and downs of life.[55]

سودا ہے بے خلش یہ زخود رفتگی کی راہ ؛ کانٹا نہ پایں ان کے فلک نے چبھو دیا

The ideal of asceticism along with mysticism proved to be a great source of strength to a generation of people who suffered heavily in an age marked by continuous political disorders, military activity, financial crisis and insecurity and generally adverse circumstances. The poets who had personally experienced those calamities in Delhi portray the contemporary attitude of seeking shelter in mystic contentment and in the ideal of asceticism. Such an attitude, it may be added, is more marked in Delhi poetry than in poetry written in the atmosphere of political stability and affluence of Awadh.

The Spirit of Toleration

Religion though enjoying a predominant place in the lives of the people remained largely free from bigotry, fanaticism and communalism and despite the diversity of religious beliefs and practices an electic and tolerant atmosphere prevailed in the eighteenth century. While Urdu poetry of the period gives free expression to the spirit of the age, certain liberal writings, including the works of Mirza Jan-i-janan played a significant role in furthering the liberal trends and in bringing the Muslims and Hindus ideologically closer. Mirza considered the Vedas as divinely inspired and did not include the pre-Islamic Hindu Gods, Rama and Krishna among infidels.[56] He, however, had no sympathy with the unbelievers who continued to follow their faith after the advent of Islam. In spite of this obvious relapse into the conventional attitude.[57] Mirza's approach to Hinduism was certainly an improvement on the orthodox view point prevalent in his times. He even commended a large following of Hindu disciples[58] who were interested in Persian and Urdu poetry. In keeping with the iconoclastic tradition of the Urdu ghazal, he points out:

> Keep aloof from the quarrel between the
> rosary and the holy thread
> United as they are in entwined relationship.[59]

کوئی تسبیح اور زنار کے جھگڑے میں مت بولو ؎ کہ آخر ایک ہیں آپس میں دونوں بیچ رشتا ہے

Religion in its simple, rather than its ritualistic aspects, finds favour with the poets as well as their society. Common beliefs and practices, saint worship and celebration of various *urs* remained the most popular aspects of the religious life in spite of condemnation by orthodox ulama and scholars. The saints and martyrs infact possessed a more meaningful place in the religious life of the Muslims than the puritanical details of the Shariat. Nazir Akbarabadi thus describes with great fervour the urs of Dataganj Bakhsh,[60] Salim Chishti[61] and the birth of Lord Krishna.[62] The guardians of the Shariat and of the public morals, namely, the Shaikh and the Zahid, form a subject of constant ridicule and condemnation in Urdu poetry. Mir, exposing the bigotry and hypocrisy practised by them in the name of religion writes:

I the intoxicated one, am not concerned with
    Shariat
I simply forced the Shaikh to silence in the
    mosque.[63]

مجھ مست کو کیا نسبت اے میر مسائل سے ۔ منہ شیخ کا مسجد میں رک رک کے سل ڈالا

All religions preach the same ideals, faith in God, brotherly love and humanitarianism, only the path to reach them is different, the destination is the same. God manifests himself everywhere, in elements of nature, air and water and in different religions, the Bible, the Hindu scriptures and the Holy Quran.[64] Mir points out in the eclectic spirit of his age:

Islam owes its greatness to the presence of
    kufr (unbelief)
The sacred thread lends its beauty to the
    Muslim rosary.[65]

کفر کچھ چاہئے اسلام کی رونق کے لئے ۔ حسن زنار ہے تسبیح سلیمانی کا

True religion is to be identified with the concept of love of God, rather than with futile debates on ritualistic aspects of religion. For a truly religious man, there is no difference between Ram or Rahim, for God is neither Hindu nor Muslim. Mosques and temples are mere creation of men.

Dard, you may omit the pilgrimage to
    Kaaba and the temple
But do try to win the heart of the
    down trodden.[66]

کعبہ کو کبھی نہ جائیے دیر کو کبھی نہ جائیے ۔ دل ہیں کسو کے درد یاں ہو وے تو راہ لیجئے

Laying stress on the concept of religious universality, Hatim points out:

Be it a temple or a Kaaba, I found neither
believer nor a non-believer,
There was God and only God in both places.[67]

کعبہ و دیر میں حاتم بخدا غیر خدا ؎ کوئی کافر نہ کوئی ہم نے مسلماں دیکھا

Condemning the bigotry of the religious classes Sauda writes:

O Shaikh you have demolished the temple and
built a mosque
But have you thought of healing the wound
inflicted on the Brahmin's heart.[68]

توڑ کر بت خانے کو مسجد بنا کی تو نے شیخ ؎ برہمن کے دل کی بھی کچھ فکر ہے تعمیر کا

Sauda would prefer the fires of hell rather than subject himself to questioning by the orthodox.

O munkir and Nakeer I would prefer going to hell
Than indulge in question and answer with you.[69]

دوزخ مجھے قبول ہے اے منکر و نکیر ؎ لیکن نہیں دماغ سوال و جواب کا

The poetry of Mir, Sauda and Mir Dard give expression to the religious ideals common to both Hinduism and Islam such as belief in one supreme being, the immortality of soul and the transient character of the mundane world and the futility of things material. The spirit of goodwill and respect shown for each other's faith, coupled with the activities of the Hindu and Muslim preachers who taught the message of mutual love and individual piety combined to create an atmosphere of toleration in Hindu-Muslim relations.

Shia-Sunni Polemics

The prevailing spirit of toleration was occasionally marred by sectarian differences within Hinduism and Islam.[70] As regards Islam though a large number of intellectuals, reformers, poets, scholars and sufi saints were concerned with the strengthening of Muslim society and freeing it from sectarian differences, the Shia-Sunni polemics continued to plague Muslim religious life, The Shia-Sunni beliefs and prejudices as reflected in the poetry of the period give a fairly clear picture of the nature and extent of these differences among the Muslims. Among the poets, Sauda and Mir (the latter possessed the zeal of a convert) were staunch shites while Mir Dard and Mazhar Jan-i-janan were orthodox Sunnis. But for occasional instances of fanaticism as in the case of Sauda's satire on Shah Walliullah, they give voice to the broader ideal of toleration and universal harmony in religious matters.

Sauda and Mir in a number of verses and long marsiahs express their faith in shite beliefs.

> I am a partisan neither to Shias, nor to Sunnis
> I know, however, that there are only twelve Imams
> All other Imams are like the imam of a rosary.[71]

مجھ کو ہر چند نہیں شیعہ و سنّی سے کام ؎ پر یہ سمجھا ہوں کہ اس دور میں ہیں بارہ امام

اُن سوا ہو جو کوئی ہے وہ امام تسبیح

In an other verse, Sauda eulogizes the twelve imams revered by the Shias:

> O Sauda, the holy twelve (Imams) are my lords
> in both the worlds
> For me, the dust of their doorstep is more
> valuable than gold.[72]

ہیں جو والی میرے بارہ دو جہاں میں سودا ؎ خاکِ در ان کی سمجھتا ہوں میں زر سے بہتر

Mir like Sauda expresses his firm faith in Shite religion. To him the status enjoyed by Ali is recognised by everyone, from the Shaikh and Syed to the Mughal. If some fool says that Ali is separate from the prophet, then who is going to believe that rogue? Dust be on the man who considers Ali and the prophet as separate, when the prophet attained *meraj*, he met Ali there.[73] At another place he points out:

> Ali is my guide, companion, helper and friend
> Ali is my Pir as well as leader,
> He is my hope and destination.[74]

ہادی علی، رفیق علی، رہنما علی ؛ یاور علی، ممد علی، آشنا علی
مرشد علی، کفیل علی پیشوا علی ؛ مقصد علی مراد علی مدّعا علی

Sauda unlike Mir did not confine himself to eulogisation of the Imams or expressing his faith in them but also satirised the Sunni point of view. He wrote a long satire on Shah Waliullah and on one Maulvi Sajid which are obvious manifestation of his own religious prejudices. Sauda lampoons Shah Waliullah for his bigoted attitude towards the Shia beliefs. According to him, the Shah's hatred for everything Shia was so intense that he would prefer to go blind rather than use the collyrium made in Isfahahan, a place inhabited by the Shias.[75] He would not hesitate from ordering a man to be hanged at the mere utterance of the name of Ali.[76] Sauda further condemns Shah Waliullah for showing admiration for Muawiyya, the rival of Husain, in whose favour he had willed that a *chauri* (flywhisk) be made of his hair after his death, to drive away the flies from the grave of Muawiyya.[77] He concludes the satire by calling Shah Waliullah a second Yazid, the murderer of Husain and his family:

> Husain is no more, otherwise he (Shah) will
> kill him again
> In fact this fool is a second Yazid himself.[78]

نہیں حسین وگرنہ کرے ابھی یہ قتل ؛ غرض جہاں میں یہ ناداں یزید کا ثانی

In another satire,[79] Sauda launches a tirade against Sunni beliefs and practices. The Sunnis rejoice at the sighting of the moon in the month of Muharram, wear rich clothes even on the day of Ashura (The tenth of

Muharram) put henna on the palms and collyrium in the eyes, instead of mourning.[80] Even the fact that Husain was martyred in this month does not stop the Sunnis from rejoicing during this period.[81]

In his satirisation of Shah Waliullah and the Sunnis, Sauda's target remained the traditional sectarian differences rather than the Shah's role as a religious reformer of the age. Sauda's close association with the court of Awadh as it emerged as the centre of Shite political power, however, might have served as an added encouragement for him to launch his attack on Shah Waliullah and the Sunni beliefs. The works and teachings of Shah Waliullah were not formally refuted by contemporary Shia theologians and scholars till the writing of the *Tuhfa-i-Ithna Ashariyya*[82] by Shah Abdul Aziz in 1789-90, almost a decade after Sauda's death. Several rebuttals of the book were written by Shia scholars and ulama, the most outstanding one was written by Maulana Syed Dildar Ali (1753-1820) on the orders of Nawab Asafuddaulah. In this surcharged atmosphere the Shia-Sunni differences were certainly sharpened but not to the extent of impairing social relations.

The leading Naqshbandi and Chishti saints of Delhi including Mir Dard, Mirza Jan-i-janan and Shah Fakharuddin adopted a liberal attitude to Shia-Sunni differences, condemning them as futile. About Shah Fakharuddin it was said that he was a Shia in the company of Shias and Sunni in the company of Sunnis. According to him a conciliatory attitude towards the Shias prevented them from indulging in *tabarra*[83] Mirza Jan-i-janan though critical of Shia beliefs, held Ali in great reverence and wrote several verses in Persian and Urdu in his praise.[84]

> Tell the rosary of the name of Ali
> Many many thanks for giving us a learned and wise Imam.[85]

علی کے ناؤں کی تسبیح ورد کر منگا ئے ہزار شکر کہ دانا امام پایا ہے

According to Mirza for a true Muslim belief in tauhid, in the prophet and the profession of faith are important fundamentals of Islam, rather than sectarian differences and the salvation of a Muslim depended on the above beliefs.[86] Religion remained a matter of personal belief and it rarely impaired personal relationships or social ties. Mir Dard and Mirza Jan-i-janan, for instance, were held in great respect by Mir and Sauda.

The latter even composed a verse condemning the assassination of Mirza by a Shia fanatic for criticising Shia veneration of tazias as *bidat* (sinful innovation) and respect shown to a piece of wood lunacy.[87]

> A wretched asportate assassinated Mazhar,
> And news of his martyrdom spread all over
> the country
> Overwhelmed with grief,
> Sauda deduced the date of his demise
> From the words, Alas Janijanan.[88]

مظہر کا ہوا جو قاتل اک مرتد شوم ؛ اور اس کی ہوئی خبر شہادت کی عموم
تاریخِ وفات کہی از روئے درد ؛ سودا نے کہا کہ ہائے جانِ جاناں مظلوم

The saint refused to divulge the identity of his assassin and even wished to forgive him in the best tradition of a sufi;

> An ardent lover, who failed to pray for the
> welfare of his assassin,
> Has in fact failed to pay due homage to love.[89]

آں کشتہ تیغ حق محبت ادا نہ کرد ؛ گز بہرِ دست و بازوئے قاتل دعا نہ کرد

The death of Mirza, without divulging the name of the assassin created considerable tension among the Shias and Sunnis. Mirza Najaf Khan's hand was suspected in the assassination of Mirza due to both religious and political reasons as his influence and popularity among the Rohilla Afghans[90] was deeply resented in Irani circles, while the regime of Najaf Khan remained extremely unpopular among the sufi saints of Delhi[91] including Mazhar Jan-i-janan, Shah Fakharuddin and Shah Abdul Aziz. Though the evidence regarding the persecution of the Sunnis by Najaf Khan including the family of Shah Abdul Aziz is not conclusive and even legendry,[92] the political dominance of the Shia regime of Najaf Khan remained very unpopular among the sufis and the Ulama.[93] The death of Najaf Khan (1782) seems to have led to the restoration of the confidence of the sufis though polemical warfare generated by writings of Shia and Sunni scholars towards the last decade of the century became more pronounced particularly in Delhi and Lucknow.[94]

The mainstream of the religious life during the second half of the eighteenth century was marked by the spirit of tolerance, mutual goodwill and an eclectic outlook which was shared by a cross section of religious groups and sects all over the country. The writings of a Dutch traveller, Stavoranius who visited India from 1765 to 1776 on the religious characteristics of the people may be noted:

> "These three distinct nations, the moors (Muslims), the gentoos (Hindus) and the Parsees whose religion is very different, yet exercised great toleration and indulgence in this respect towards one another. . . . no one is molested on account of his religion, they may be seen together in and near the river, offering up, their prayer, each to that being whom he adores, without any marks of derision or contempt being shown by any one. . . ".[95]

Twining visiting India is the last decade of the century similarly, did not see any communal bitterness. About Varanasi he writes that relations between the "haughty Musalman and the humble Hindoo" were peaceful.[96]

NOTES

1. Mir Dard, *Diwan*, p. 27
2. For a detailed study of these movements see V.P.S. Raghuvanshi, *Indian Society in the Eighteenth Century*, New Delhi, 1969, pp. 143-44.
3. *Ibid.*
4. F.H. Buchanan, *Antiquities, Topography, Statistics etc. of Eastern India*, edited, Martin Montgomery, Volume I, p. 501, footnote.
5. Asim Roy, *The Islamic Syncretistic Tradition in Bengal*, New Jersey, 1983, p. 143.
6. Sukumar Sen, *History of Bengali Literature*, New Delhi, 1960, pp. 158-160.
7. Satish Chandra, "Cultural and Political Role of Delhi, 1765-1725" in R.E. Frykenberg, (ed.), *op. cit.*, p. 210.
8. Khafi Khan, *Muntakhab ul Lubab*, p. 663; *Siyar* II, p. 8.
9. Khafi Khan, *Muntakhab ul Lubab*, pp. 940, 947.
10. Satish Chandra, 'Jizyah and the state during the 17th Century', *Journal of Economic and Social History of the Orient*, Volume XII, Leiden, 1969, p. 340.
11. T.D. Broughton, *Letters from a Mahratta Camp*, London, 1813, pp. 239-240; J.N. Sarkar, *Sindhia As Regent*, p. 49; A.A. Rizvi, *A History of Sufism in India*, New Delhi, 1983, Volume II, p. 284.

12. Firaqi, *Waqa-i-Alam Shahi*, pp. 56-57.

13. B.H. Badley, 'Jagjivandas and the Hindu Reformers' *Indian Antiquary*, VII, 1879, p. 289.

14. B.N. Goswami and J.S. Grewal, *The Mughals and the Sikh Rulers and Vaishnawas of Pindori*, Simla, 1969, Document XII, pp. 172-173.

15. *Ibid*, Documents XXIV, XXVI, XXXV, pp. 228-29, 236, 272.

16. Khafi, Khan, *Muntakhab ul Lubab*, 755, *Siyar*, II, pp. 65-66.

17. *Akhbarat-i-Darbar-i-Mulla*, J.S. Sitamau transcripts, pp. 105, 282, quoted in, Alam, Muzaffar, 'Sikh Uprising Under Banda Bahadur', *Studies in History*, 1979, p. 204; Irvine, *Later Mughals*, New Delhi, 1971, (Reprint), Volume I, pp. 96-97.

18. Khafi Khan, *Op cit.* pp. 884, 867.

19. C.A. Bayly, 'The Prehistory of Communalism'. Religious Conflict in India, 1700-1860, in *Modern Asian Studies*, April, 1985, p. 202, sees little difference between riots of 18th century and those in U.P. and Bengal in 1920s and 1930-40s. The riots in the earlier period though not wholly devoid of socio-economic motivations lacked in political objectives. No power or political group during this period used communal or sectarian slogans to rally support for political advancement, a characteristic that became a common feature of the riots in the 20th century.

20. Ziaul Hasan Faruqi, 'Orthodoxy and Heterodoxy in Muslim India', *Islam and the Modern Age*, Volume X, No. 1, 1979, pp. 11-12.

21. Shah Waliullah, *Fuyuzl Harmayn*, Urdu Translation, Syed Zahiruddin Ahmad, Delhi, p. 89.

22. Shah Waliullah, *Hujjatullah Baligha*, Urdu Translation, Muhammad Abdul Haq Haqqam, Karachi, Volume I, pp. 124-128.

23. Shah Waliullah, *Muktubat*, Rampur, MS. quoted, S.A.A. Rizvi, *Shah Waliullah and his times*, Canberra, 1980, p. 227. According to Rizvi, these injunctions have been deleted by K.A. Nizami in his translation of the Maktubat, Aligarh, 1950.

24. S.A.A. Rizvi, *Shah Abdul Aziz, Puritanism, Sectarian Polemics and Jihad*, pp. 109-110.

25. A. Schimmel, 'Reflections on Popular Muslim Poetry' in *Contributions to Asian Studies*, Volume XVIII, Leiden, 1982, p. 18.

26. Mirza Mazhar Jan-i-janan in Qureshi, Abdur Razzaq, *Mirza Jan-i-Janan Aur Unka kalam*, Bombay, 1961, p. 271.

27. Mir Dard, *Ilmulkitab*, Delhi, 1892, pp. 106, 187-188.

28. Syed Nuruddin Husaini Fakhri, *Fakhrul Talibin*, MS, p. 13, quoted, K.A. Nizami, *Tarikhi-i-Mashaikh Chisht*, Delhi, 1984, Vol. V, p. 230.

29. Mirza Mazhar Jan-i-janan, *Mirza Mazhar Jan-i-janan Ke Khutoot*, edited, Khaliq Anjum, Delhi, 1962, No. 12, pp. 88-89.

30. Qazi Muhammad Bashiruddin, *Malfuzat-i-Shah Abdul Aziz*, Meerut, p. 78.

31. Mir Dard, *Nala-i-Dard*, p. 36; Shah Waliullah, *Wasiyat Nama*, Urdu translation Syed Zahiruddin, Delhi, 1899, p. 65; Dargah Quli Khan, *Muraqqa-i-Dehli*, Urdu translation Nurul Hasan Ansari, Delhi, 1982, pp. 142-143.

32. G. Anawati, 'Philosophy, Theology and Mysticism' in J. Schacht and C.E. Bosworth, (eds.), *The Legacy of Islam*, Oxford, 1974, p. 368, dismisses the history of sufism from the 16th century onwards as decadent. Similar views are expressed in J.S. Trimingham, *The Sufi Orders in Islam*, Oxford, 1971.

33. Mrs Meer Hasan Ali, *Observations on the Mussulmans of India*, Delhi, 1973, Volume II, pp. 247-300.

34. Mir Dard, *Diwan*, p. 51.

35. *Ibid.*, p. 52.

36. *Ibid.*, p. 115.
37. Mirza Jan-i-Janan in A. Qureshi, *op. cit.*, p. 258.
38. Zameeruddin M. Siddiqi, 'The Resurgence of the Chishti Silsila in the Punjab during the Eighteenth Century, *Proceeding of Indian History Congress*, 1970, pp. 408-420; K.A. Nizami, *Tarikh-i-Mashaikh Chisht*, V, pp. 183-249.
39. Mir Dard, *Diwan*, p. 21.
40. *Ibid.*, p. 68
41. *Ibid.*, p. 40.
42. *Ibid.*, p. 25.
43. Mir Taqi Mir, *Kulliyat*, I, p. 19.
44. *Ibid.*, p. 130; also pp. 65, 242, 357, 391.
45. *Ibid.*, p. 193.
46. Husain Ibn Mansur (857-922) known as al Hallaj a 'reader of hearts' was judged and sentenced to death as a heretic in Baghdad in 922. See, Louis Massignon, *The Passion of Al Hallaj, Mystic and Martyr of Islam*, Translated Herbert Manson, Princeton, New Jersey, 1982, 4 Vols.
47. Mir Taqi Mir, *Kulliyat*, I, p. 338; also Sauda, *Kulliyat*, II, p. 241, Hatim, *Diwanzada*, p. 83.
48. Hatim, *Diwanzada*, p. 43.
49. Sauda, *Kulliyat*, I, p. 400.
50. Mir Dard, *Diwan*, p. 23.
51. *Ibid.*, p. 98.
52. Hatim, *Diwanzada*, p. 147.
53. Mir, *Kulliyat*, I, p. 513.
54. *Ibid.*, II, 385-386.
55. Sauda, *Kulliyat*, I, p. 400.
56. Mirza Jan-i-janan, *Khutoot*, No. 14, pp. 94-95.
57. Y. Friedmann, 'Medieval views on Indian Religions', *JAOS*, Connecticut, 1975, p. 221.
58. Mirza Jan-i-janan, *Khutoot*, No. 36, p. 143.
59. Mirza Jan-i-janan, in A.R. Qureshi, *Mirza Jan-i-janan*, p. 272.
60. Nazir Akbarabadi, *Kulliyat*, pp, 49-50.
61. *Ibid.*, p. 53.
62. *Ibid.*, pp. 55-56.
63. Mir Taqi Mir, *Kulliyat*, I, p. 290.
64. Hatim, *Diwanzada*, p. 34.
65. Mir, *Kulliyat*, I, p. 20.
66. Mir Dard, *Diwan*, p. 117.
67. Hatim, *Diwanzada*, p. 106.
68. Sauda, *Kulliyat*, I, p. 391. Munkir an angel who with his companion abgel Nakeer interrogates the dead in the grave.
69. *Ibid.*, p. 386.
70. V.P.S. Raghuvanshi, *Indian Society in the Eighteenth Century*, pp. 112-116.
71. Sauda, *Kulliyat*, II, p. 148.
72. *Ibid.*, I. p. 455
73. Mir Taqi Mir, *Kulliyat*, I, p. 258; also II, p. 389.
74. *Ibid.*, II, p. 390.
75. Sauda, *Kulliyat*, I, p. 222.
76. *Ibid.*
77. *Ibid.*

78. *Ibid.*, p. 223.
79. *Ibid.*, pp. 223-225.
80. *Ibid.*, p. 223.
81. *Ibid.*
82. S.A.A. Rizvi, *Shah Abdul Aziz*, pp. 255-256.
83. *Ibid.*, pp. 39, 80-81.
84. Qudratullah Qasim, *Majmua-i-Naghz*, II, p. 199.
85. Mirza Jan-i-janan in Qureshi, *Mirza Mazhar*, p. 272.
86. Mirza Jan-i-janan, *Khutoot*, No. 18, p. 105.
87. Mirza Lutf Ali, *Gulshan-i-Hind*, Delhi, 1906, p. 217.
88. Sauda, *Kulliyat*, II, p. 152.
89. Maulvi Naimullah Baharaichi, *Mamlaat-i-Mazhariya*, Kanpur, 1275, p. 14, quoted Qureshi, A., *op. cit.*, p. 70.
90. Mirza Jan-i-janan, *Khutoot*, No. 74, pp. 195-196.
91. *Ibid.*, Mushafi, *Tazkirah-i-Hind*, p. 248, Ghaziuddin Khan Nizam, *Manaqib-i-Fakhriya*, MS, p. 28, quoted in K.A. Nizami, *Tarikh-i-Mashaikh Chisht*, p. 220.
92. S.A.A. Rizvi, *Shah Abdul Aziz*, p. 83.
93. Mushafi, *Tazkirah-i-Hindi*, p. 248; Mirza Jan-i-janan, *Khutoot*, No. 34, p. 139.
94. S.A.A. Rizvi, *Shah Abdul Aziz*, pp. 356-470.
95. John Splinter Stavorinus, *Voyage to the East Indies*, London, 1798, Vol. III, p. 6.
96. T. Twining, *Travels*, p. 332.

6

URBAN LIFE

These lonely and deserted lanes and streets
Where once the abode of those who possessed great wealth.[1]

اڑتی ہے خاک شہر کی گلیوں میں اب جہاں ؎ سونا لیا ہے گودوں میں بھر کر وہیں سے ہم

The mid-eighteenth century witnessed a steady decline of the imperial cities of Delhi and Agra, leaving a deep imprint on the various facets of urban life. Delhi, suffered repeated invasions and pillaging as it continued to be coveted as the seat of imperial power by the contending powers throughout the eighteenth century. The large scale emigration from Delhi, and to a lesser extent from Agra, to the neighbouring states of Farrukhabad and Awadh may serve as an index to their declining fortunes. The picture of desolation and ruin drawn by the poets of Delhi refers to the most turbulent phase in Delhi's history lasting from 1739 to 1760. A time when the capital lived under the shadow of constant invasion, massacre and atrocities perpetrated by the armies of Nadir Shah, Ahmad Shah Abdali, the Jats and the Marathas on the population of Delhi. The chaotic and uncertain conditions led to an exodus from Delhi which chiefly comprised the nobles, scholars, artists and poets who left the capital in search for security and livelihood in more peaceful regions. The city however showed a remarkable resilience. The desolation was a temporary phase and Delhi recovered much of its economic stability in the last two decades of the century. Socially, however, the capital lost much of its old gaiety and aristocratic splendour of the age of Muhammad Shah although it continued to be resided in by wealthy nobles and traders.

Agra also suffered the fate of Delhi, though not to the same extent, as desolation was confined to aristocratic, localities lying between the fort and the Tajmahal.[2] Trade and commerce continued to flourish in Agra during the Jat and Maratha occupation of the city while many rich and noble families settled down there to avoid the troubles in Delhi.[3] No general decline of the cities of Delhi and Agra can, therefore, be assumed on the basis of the evidence of the poets. Sauda and Mir's cries of anguish at the fall of Delhi in fact highlight the decline of the old nobility and the professional groups dependent on it. As regards other regions, decline was confined to cities lying west of Delhi[4] while large cities such as Lucknow, Banaras and Murshidabad flourished on the eastern side of the capital.

Delhi and Agra

The poets express great grief at the ruin and havoc caused by the invading armies in Delhi: great palaces and mansions lay in ruins, bazaars, khanqahs and mosques lay deserted while the citizens suffered from a deep sense of insecurity and fear. Mir and Sauda not merely narrate the contemporary situation but, also give expression to their nostalgia about the conditions which had preceded this decline.

> Houses, inns and all other places bear a deserted look
> All friends and companions appear to have departed.[5]

ہیں مکان وسرا وجا خالی ؛ یارسب کوچ کرگئے شاید

Similar sentiments are expressed in another verse of Mir.

> Here lived the wazir in his palaces in great pomp and grandeur
> With his departure the palaces have also fallen into decay.[6]

کیاکیا مکان شاہ نشیں تھے وزیر کے ؛ وہ اٹھ گیا تو یہ بھی گرے بیٹھ ڈھ گئے

Sauda laments the desolation of Delhi and narrates the consequent impact on the life of the people at great length. The ruin of the city, according to him was such that even the most heartless person might lose his senses (in grief). The reign of terror is let loose in Delhi, houses are confiscated, soldiers loot and kill people while lawless elements take full advantage of the chaos to further their nefarious activities.[7] In another verse describing the desolation of the city, the poet points out, "There is no house from which the Jackal's cry cannot be heard" while the city's mosques remain deserted, and lamps unlit in the evenings.[8]

> Houses that still stand are without a fire-place or a mill stone
> Lamps are seen burning, only in one house in a thousand,
> And donkeys bray in places
> Where in former times
> Men sat and enjoyed the songs of spring.[9]

کسی کے یاں نہ رہا آسیا ہے تا بہ اجاغ ؎ ہزار گھر میں کہیں ایک گھر جلے ہے چراغ
سو کیا چراغ وہ گھر ہے گھروں کے غم سے داغ ؎ اور ان مکانوں میں ہر سمت رینگتے ہیں الاغ
جہاں بہاریں سنتے تھے بیٹھ کر ہنڈول

The once breathtakingly beautiful mansions are devoid of past grandeur. Not a single lamp is lit in a house where huge chandeliers were once hung. The only remnants of past glory seem to be the huge mirrors lying in the debris.[10] The gardens surrounding the mansions are also in ruins, bulbuls no longer sing sweet songs among flowers, only shrill cries of crows and kites may now be heard among fallen pillars.[11]

> O Jahanabad, you, who were like the heart of a lover
> Had done nothing to deserve such a fate
> To be obliterated like an impression that never existed.[12]

جہاں آباد تو کب اس ستم کے قابل تھا ؎ مگر کبھو کسی عاشق کا یہ نگر دل تھا
کہ یوں اٹھا دیا گویا کہ نقشِ باطل تھا

Mir shares with Sauda, similar sentiments about the fate of Delhi.

> Jahanabad now lies in ruins
> Otherwise there was a house at every step.[13]

اب خرابا ہوا جہاں آباد ؎ ورنہ ہر اک قدم پہ یاں گھر تھا

Hatim, who lived in Delhi throughout his life, shares with Mir and Sauda sorrow at the desolation of Delhi in the following verse:

> O Hatim, the times are most depressing
> The world, losing its luster, is like a garden
> Without water and flowers with dew therein.[14]

عجب بے رونق اے حاتم ہوا ہے اس زمانے کی ؛ چمن بے آب و گل بے رنگ اور نایاب ہے شبنم

Dard who shared the grief of the decline of Delhi with his fellow citizens writes in sufistic tones:

> The flower that for long adorned a garden
> Is now lying dead in dust and bushes.[15]

جلتا ہے اب پڑا خس و خاشاک میں ملا ؛ وہ گل کہ ایک عمر چمن کا چراغ تھا

or again,

> Wandering through the ruins, I hear people exclaim,
> Only some time ago there were gardens and houses here.[16]

گزروں ہوں جس خرابے پہ کہتے ہیں واں کے لوگ ؛ ہے کوئی دن کی بات یہ گھر تھا یہ باغ تھا

Certain significant features emerge from the poets' narration of the ruin and desolation of Delhi. Sauda wrote his *Shahr Ashob* around 1757 just before he left Delhi for Farrukhabad,[17] a time when the capital had just witnessed a holocaust at the hands of Ahmad Shah Abdali. This is clear from his account of the confiscation of houses, the activities of the soldiers, the empty half ruined houses whose occupants had either taken shelter in another part of the city or migrated to one of the neighbouring states.[18] Mir had similarly experienced the pillaging of the city at the hands of the various contending powers including the invasion of Abdali in 1756-57 and 1760-1761 of which he gives a graphic account in his autobiography.[19] Hatim and Dard similarly witnessed each successive attack on the capital and saw the city reduced to ruins in a short period:

> The whole country is in the grip of unprecedented riots and mischief
> There is no place of refuge left, except in God's mercy.[20]

ایسی ہوا بہی ہے کہ چاروں طرف فساد ہے   جز سایۂ خدا کہیں دارالاماں نہیں

The poets account of the desolation and ruin of Delhi and its surrounding territories substantiate contemporary sources which speak of the desolation of Delhi and cities lying west of the capital in the middle of the eighteenth century. The areas in the immediate vicinity of Delhi were marked by lawlessness to the extent that peasants carry their arms with them to the field.[21] In the villages surrounding Delhi, little cultivation was done while women did not dare to venture out to draw water from the wells as they remained filled with corpses.[22]

Mir who travelled to a place called Nasang in Karnal[23] (1772-73) paints a similar picture of ruin and desolation in the region, lying Southwest of Delhi. On his way to Nasang, Mir describes the condition of Shahadara, Meerut and Ghaziabad towns which lay in a state of desolation. Mir found the town of Shahadara in ruins, the nobles in desperate circumstances, houses destroyed and markets deserted.[24] He refers to the prevailing sense of insecurity because of constant threat of Sikh attacks.[25] Meerut and Ghaziabad suffered a similar fate, villages lay deserted, houses stood with half crumbling walls, infested with mosquitos and poisonous insects, reptiles and stray dogs roam about in search of food.[26] The ruling classes and men of wealth in these towns, as in case of Delhi, seemed to have suffered heavy losses. The whole *basti* or locality in one of these towns (Nasang), writes Mir, wears a deserted look with only a few havelis or huts left which are inhabited by sickly occupants.[27] The whole locality, Mir regrets, because of the ruin of the nobles, is in occupation of low born people. Mosques are found in a state of disrepair, with no *Khatib* or Imam as very few people are left in the town to come for prayers. The local market is similarly deserted with only a few commodities to sell.[28]

Mir's description of these territories in the immediate vicinity of Delhi indicates large scale devastation of both urban and rural areas. The towns, qasbahs and ganjs that shared the fate of Delhi, suffered economic hardships in the form of disruption of the movement of trade, shortage of supplies and unemployment to a large number of artisans and professionals whose constant worry centred around the issue of procuring daily bread. Even the local bania, remained under heavy stress as it was difficult to get supplies for daily needs.[29]

> Be thankful to eat lentils
> For who has tasted the delicacy of meat[30]

ماش کی دال کا نہ کرے گلا ؛ گوشت یاں ہے کبھو کسو کو ملا

The *bania* then advises Mir to go and buy a goat. But where is the money to buy one when there is none even to procure cheap vegetables.[31] In the rural areas a similar situation prevailed. The destruction of cultivation and constant threat of movement of armies and activities of the thugs added to the miseries of the peasant who like the urban population lived under constant threat of starvation and debt to the local money lender.[32]

> We (peasants) take a loan even before the crop is harvested
> Yet the money-lender lists us among thieves for non-payment.[33]

فصل ہونے ابھی نہیں پائی ؛ پیشگی سب سے قرض لے کھائی
جس سے جھوٹے ہوئے ہیں ہم دس بار ؛ چوٹا وہ کہے ہے ساہوکار

Mir and Sauda's verses clearly speak of the great desolation of Delhi and its surrounding towns and *qasbahs* as well as rural areas in the mid-eighteenth century. By 1740s this had resulted in the dislocation of trade because of the prevailing lawlessness and insecurity in the Delhi Doab — Agra region. The activities of the Jats and Mewatis in the tracts south of Delhi restricted the movements of goods in the region around the capital.[34] Again, the intention of Hodges in visiting Delhi was thus frustrated partly due to the movement of the armies of Mirza Shafi in the environs of Agra and also because the route to Delhi remained unsafe.[35] In this situation, trade links between the trading towns of Gujarat were severed with the heart land of imperial cities of Agra and Delhi thus, adversely affecting movement of trade on the old routes. Hodges travelling from Lucknow to Agra in the early 1780s speaks of ruined cultivation, deserted villages and systematic brigandage by the Mewatis and Gujars[36] which was a constant threat to the movement of trade. Several verses of Nazir refer to the activities of these lawless elements and its impact on trade in the Agra region.

Highway robbery has struck terror in the hearts of traders
Kotwals and Chowkidars are equally helpless
While boatmen refuse to cross the river from one ghat to the other.[37]

لوٹیں ہیں گرد و پیش جو قزاق راہ مار ؏ بیوپاری آتے جاتے نہیں ڈرتے زینہار
کتوال روئیں خاک اڑاتے ہیں چوکی دار ملاحوں کا بھی کام نہیں چلتا ہے میرے یار
ناویں ہیں گھاٹ گھاٹ کی سب وار پار بند

In another verse he points to the same problem with a touch of sarcasm.

Those travelling with their merchandize are human beings
And those who strangulate them are human too.[38]

چلتا ہے آدمی ہی مسافر ہوکے مال ؏ اور آدمی ہی مارے ہے پھانسی گلے میں ڈال

Agra, like several other cities around Delhi suffered not merely from the breakdown of trade due to plundering activities in the region by hostile armies,[39] but its population also suffered extreme economic hardships which find expression in Nazir's verses:

Be they noblemen or artisans, all are helpless for want of livelihood
The wind of disaster seems to have blown away every thing.[40]

کیا چھوٹے کام والے وہ کیا پیشہ ور نجیب ؏ روزی کے آج ہاتھ سے عاجز ہیں سب غریب

Unemployment in the city of Agra was not confined to merely soliders or artisans, points out Nazir, but extended to no less than thirty six professions.[41]

Men of all professions bewail their fate
Blacksmiths and Goldsmiths beat their breasts in despair
Be they merchants, traders, drapers or grocers
Business means profit no longer,
This is not the story of one or two
No less than thirty six professions suffer.[42]

مارے ہیں ہاتھ ہاتھ پہ سب یاں کے دستکار ؏ اور جتنے پیشہ ور ہیں سو روتے ہیں زار زار
کوٹے ہے تن لوہار تو پیٹے ہے سر سنار ؏ کچھ ایک دو کے کام کا رونا نہیں ہے یار
چھتیس پیشے والوں کے ہیں کاروبار بند

No one in Agra, continues Nazir, is leading a life of comfort, leave alone affluence while the whole town lies desolate and prostrate.

> All the gardens in Agra are lying desolate
> Without thorns, not to speak of fruits and flowers
> Fruit trees stand scorched and dried and alleys covered with dust
> In short, all are in the grip of a devastating autumn.[43]

ہیں باغ جتنے یاں کے سو ایسے پڑے ہیں خوار ؎ کانٹے کا نام ان میں نہیں پھول در کنار
سوکھے ہوئے کھڑے ہیں درختانِ میوہ دار ؎ کیاری میں خاک دھول روِش پر اڑے غبار
ایسی خزاں کے ہاتھ ہوئی ہے بہار بند

There is no one in Agra who does not suffer from frustration while the thought of procuring bread seems to be overpowering with all, from the ordinary soul to the nobleman.

The above quoted verses of Nazir on Agra's distress and desolation refer to the period of acute scarcity and famine in the years 1781 and 1782 to 1784 and therefore, need not be generalized to cover the entire history of the city during the eighteenth century. The foreign travellers who depicted desolation and banditry on the high road to Agra did not notice the fertile tract lying south of the city which was well cultivated in the 1790s, also benefiting from the continuous pull of the urban market during the period.[44] Temporary economic hardships caused by the pillaging of the invading armies or famine conditions did not imply an overall collapse of trade or economy in the region. Trade and credit relations infact condinued[45] despite the repeated lootings of the northern cities by various contending forces. Several leading banking houses, repeatedly fleeced by invaders like Nadir Shah and Ahmad Shah and the Marathas, quickly regained their former strength although they avoided transactions with the imperial house.[46] The Jagat Seths had a correspondent in Agra within a short time after Abdali's invasion in 1759. Another great pan Indian commercial house, Arunji Nathji Tiwari of Surat, which had been serving the cross country route since 1720s emerged, unscathed from the holocaust. Its agents were again sending lakhs of rupees from Bengal overland to Surat and Bombay before the mid-1770s.[47]

Even in Delhi which witnessed a large scale exodus of people from the city from mid-century onwards that left many of its localities deserted, contemporary accounts refer to many other residential areas in the 1780s including two dozen flourishing bazaars.[48] The period also witnessed the increasing power of such economic groups as traders, bankers, and petty businessmen who made huge profits in the prevailing conditions. These groups enjoyed increasing authority and power in the urban life which earned them contempt and condemnation of the poets and the intellectuals who saw the rise of these 'low born' elements with great dismay.

> In the present age people have lost maturity of judgement
> What a pity! Good fortune favours the mean and the low born.[49]

رہی نہ پختگی عالم میں دورِ خامی ہے ؎ ہزار حیف کمینوں کا چرخ حامی ہے

The bankers, *sarrafs* and jewellers infact amassed great wealth and power during this period as the declining fortunes of the imperial government had made the monarchs and the nobles heavily dependent on the bankers who paid them loans for performing their military obligations.

Incessant warfare and the great desolation of Delhi disrupted law and order, weakened the administration leaving a deep imprint on the life in the capital. These aspects are mirrored in the poetry of the age, especially in that of Sauda who as a critic and satirist exposes the ills of the contemporary society. The prevailing corruption among public officials as well as corresponding loss of faith among the people towards the authorities do not escape the poet's attention. His satire on the Kotwal of Delhi well portrays the life in the capital in the turbulent years from 1757 to 1759.

Sauda regrets at the breakdown of law and order in the city and recalls the times when even a petty crime never escaped punishment.[50] When the capital used to be peaceful and the people happy and contended, not a single thief was to be found while the Kotwal of the city had nothing to do with bribery. But now continues the poet, in any direction one might look, there is no scarcity of thugs and thieves with the result that it is no longer safe even to walk down the main street, without the lurking fear of being apprehended by one of them.[51] The poet accuses the Kotwal of having joined with the thieves in the business as he does not hesitate in accepting bribes or in taking a share in the loot surreptitiously. Taking into account the obvious exaggeration of the satire, the real objective of the poet can hardly be missed which was to expose the weakness of the administration. Contemporary sources refer to the corruption of the chief of the city police who was found guilty of shielding the burglars and sharing their spoils.[52] The same Kotwal, Faulad Khan, seems to be the subject of Sauda's satirization.[53] A number of verses in the satire points to the inability and helplessness of the local authorities to check the miscreants. In the words of the Kotwal himself:

> Whom am I to punish or abuse?
> Nobody today can claim to be free of corruption[54]

کس کو ماروں میں کس کو دوں گالی ؛ چوری کرنے سے کون ہے خالی

The 'justification' of the authorities regarding the corruption rampant within their own ranks is again personified in the kotwal who declares:

> Even the house of God is not spared by thieves
> How was the Kotwal to remain unaffected?[55]

مچ رہا ہے اب اس طرح کا سانگ ؛ ہے خدا کے بھی گھر میں چور کی تھانگ

کریں انصاف اب جوان و پیر ؛ کیا ہے اس میں بھلا مری تقصیر

The satire on the Kotwal of Delhi does not confine itself to criticizing the individual corruption of Shidi Faulad but well extends its scope to exposing the breakdown of administrative machinery, the resulting lawlessness and corruption prevalent in Sauda's times. The state of law and order in Delhi during the 1750s[56] seemed to have crossed even the limits set by medieval standards so as to provoke Sauda into satirizing the prevailing situation in the capital. These turbulent conditions were bound to adversely affect the social, economic and cultural activity in the capital. According to Sauda, each night in the city is like waiting for the doomsday while no one dares to sleep in peace. Even the holy Shaikh can not concentrate on his prayers because of the fear of lawless elements.[57] The dogs bark at the slightest movement so loudly as to even awaken the dead from their sleep. In such an atmosphere, social gatherings have lost the old glitter and gaiety. Even those who venture to go out, they go fully armed as if moving to the battle front.[58] The fear of lawless elements make it virtually impossible for people to attend even public prayers in the mosques. In frustration no one pays heed to the call of religion, if the Mullah gives the call for prayer, they gag him saying, "Be quiet, what is this talk about Musalmani (Islam)?"[59]

Sauda's account of the life in the capital pertains to an age marked by continuous political upheaval, military activity and economic crisis, which offer a great contrast to the life of great social and cultural activity and affluence portrayed in earlier works like Muraqqa-i-Delhi.[60] The destruction of the city of Delhi and the surrounding towns affected urban life, which changed from one of carefree affluence and frivolity to the one marked by military air noticed in most cities in Doab, Awadh and Agra, being most "striking in Delhi".[61] Though in most cities, markets and bazaars continued to attract crowds, most people preferred to carry with them arms of some sort.[62] As regards Delhi, its decline in the mid-eighteenth century remained a subject of great distress to the poets, from Hatim and Sauda to Mir and Dard. To them it signified the ruin of a society and a way of life which had embodied the best traditions of the medieval culture. Although Delhi continued to be resided in by a considerable number of poets, sufis, scholars and traders after the departure of Mir and Sauda from the city, the old world spirit and charm seemed to be missing.

> Now nothing is left of the Mushairas, except the name
> Just a gathering of novices
> Is there any one among them
> Who my aspire to be a Mir, a Mirza Rafi or Khwajah Mir.[63]

کیا رہا ہے مشاعرے میں اب ؎ لوگ کچھ جمع آن ہوتے ہیں
میر و مرزا رفیع و خواجہ میر ؎ کتنے اک یہ جوان ہوتے ہیں

Court Culture

The Mughal court, despite its political decline, remained the school of manners for Hindustan throughout the eighteenth century. The forms of address, the conventions of behaviour and even in case of ceremonial dress other states followed the standard of Delhi. The Marathas and Jats in spite of plebian background adopted the manner and etiquette of the Delhi court. Even the French General in the service of Mahadaji Sindhia,

Ccunt Benoit dè Boine is said to have followed the life style of a Mughal noble, held his 'court' in the Mughal style where 'Nazars' were offered to him in the tradition of Mughal etiquette.[64] In spite of the troubles of the century, the pattern of Mughal court life survived and received a new lease of life not only in provincial kingdoms like Awadh, Bengal and Hyderabad but in almost all independent or autonomous states that rose on the ruins of the empire. Throughout India, the Mughal etiquette was recognised as the standard of conduct and Persian still remained the language of the diplomats and the elites.

The poets, with the exception of Nazir Akbarabadi, in view of their close proximity to the nobles, mirror to a large extent the life style of the gentry patterned on the court culture of the age though references to life of the common man, especially in the verses of Nazir, indicate a gradual emergence of a culture free of court influences.

Mir and Sauda betray great admiration for the cultural norms and life style of the nobles in the poetry composed in Delhi and Awadh. The poets at great length, describe the splendour of the noble's style of living, their houses, the interior decor, dress, values and mode of behaviour as well as their means of recreation. Sauda's description of the mansion of one of his early patrons in Delhi, namely Basant Khan[65] is not very different to that depicted in his qasidas written in praise of Nawab Shujauddaulah[66] and Asafuddaulah.[67] With the characteristic hyperbole of a qasida, Sauda eulogizes the beauty of Nawab Basant Khan's mansion. It is surrounded by extensive gardens where fountains play and birds chirp all day while his patron is seen immersed in revelry and merry making. In the same breath, Sauda eulogizes his other patrons, including Imadulmulk and Nawab Shujauddaulah and Nawab Asafuddaulah. The symbols of their affluence, splendour and dignity are visualized in their style of living: the tents are made of rich material (*Jama*) and the girders supporting them are as lovely as the twinkling stars, while the ropes holdings the tents are made of golden thread (*poat*). Again, carpets are spread inside the tents and the nawabs sit on the *masnad* surrounded by his nobles. With the object of admiring the nawabs prosperity as well as of pleasing him, Sauda exclaims, he had never seen so much gold and silver lying unheeded under the sky.[68]

Sauda links the life style of the nobles with their real or supposed prosperity as was the case with the nobles of Awadh and Delhi respectively. Sauda's belated praise for the nobles of Delhi, including his patron Imadulmulk, who was hard hit by circumstances,[69] signified the social ideal of a wealthy nobleman. Mir in this respect adopts a more realistic attitude for he refrains from indulging in the hyperbolic praise of the nobles of Delhi and even his qasida on the contemporary emperor is short and devoid of any hyperbole. He however, is full of praise for the court culture marked by pomp and show in the state of Awadh.[70] But Mir soon became dissatisfied with the court life in Awadh, its cultural norms seemed new and alien to the poet:

> Desolate Delhi was far better than Lucknow
> O that I had not come here in haste and died there.[71]

خرابہ دلّی کا وہ چند بہتر لکھنؤ سے تھا ؛ وہیں میں کاش مرجاتا سراسیمہ نہ آتا یاں

At another place, describing the entertainment given by Nawab Asafud-daulah, which included a fair amount of western entertainment, including dance, Mir writes that "it was a strange world and a strange show and atmosphere".[72]

Court culture continued to set the pattern of the life style of the nobles and the wealthy who wished to gain social recognition while the common people also aspired to follow in their footsteps. Court life in Delhi till its devastation 1739 and later in Awadh was marked by great pomp and show as well as extravagance.[73] Sauda's uninhibited account of the merry making and wine drinking on festive occasions reflect the life style of the upper classes wholly in defiance of religious prohibition against wine drinking. Those responsible for guarding the public morals turn their backs when it comes to censoring the morals of the rich, hence the zahid raises no objection if a "few drops of wine get sprinkled on his clothes".[74]

Sauda's description of merry making by nobles reflects the spirit of rejoicing and by no means highlights the problem of moral decadence of the ruling classes in the eighteenth century. A problem towards which Mir occasionally draws attention.

> The nobles' splendid and magnificent tents
> Are teeming with courtesans
> People are freely enjoying women and wine
> Having thrown all dignity to the winds
> In short, the noble is a profligate.[75]

لعل خیمہ جو ہے سپہر اساس ؎ پالیں ہیں رنڈیوں کی اس کے پاس
ہے زنا و شراب بے وسواس ؎ رعب کر بیٹھئے تہیں سے قیاس
قصّہ کوتہ رئیس ہے عیّاش

Sauda unlike Mir makes no reference to the prevailing attitude of moral laxity and the pre-occupation of the rulers and nobles, 'with women and wine' characteristics often emphasized as significant features in the decline of the Mughal nobles and the empire. This is not to suggest that since Sauda and other poets do not refer to these features, they were non-existent, for there is no dearth of evidence on this point.[76] The significant point to be noted is the fact that Sauda who wrote so extensively on the subject of decline of the empire, attached little significance to the moral decadence of the nobility as a causative factor in the fall of the empire.

Despite the predominant influence of court culture on contemporary life, social life was beginning to emerge gradually out of court circles. A beginning of this process is noticeable in Delhi where the decline of the court and the impoverishment of a large section of the nobles made it virtually impossible to continue social life on the old pattern. The decline of the old nobility brought into forefront social groups such as bankers, merchants and money-lenders who came to acquire both wealth and power in the years of 'turmoil'. The poets, while expressing anguish at the fall of the nobles or classes who claimed high descent, condemn the rise of the low born or the *Ajlaf* who comprised the various 'low' professional, trading agricultural and menial classes and who also aspired to gain in status through acquisition of wealth. All the people belonging to lower professional groups such as the cobblers, vegetable venders, grocers, sweet makers, jewellers and bankers who seemed to have made a quick buck in the 'time of troubles' receive severe condemnation of Hatim[77] and Sauda.[78]

Great contempt is expressed by Hatim in a *Shehr Ashob* written in 1729, on the rise of "the mean and the low born" people. The poet, contrary to the tradition of *Shahr Ashob* writing, does not speak of the desolation or destruction of the city because Delhi was in a flourishing condition at that time but concentrates on the rise of the trading classes at the expense of the nobility or *ashraf*. His lament on the decline of the nobles can be noted in the context of the critical financial condition of the majority of the Mughal nobles because of the growing crisis of the jagirdari system in the early decades of the century. God has been kind to these people, writes Hatim, those who once lived in poverty now roll in wealth while the great nobles have been reduced to the status of ants! What luck that men of such low origins as *ahirs*, washermen, sweet makers and darners should gain so much power and affluence. He further adds:

Strange winds seem to blow in Delhi
The nobles have fled from the cities
While the owls from the forest
Have descended on the city.[79]

عجب یہ الٹی بہی ہے گی باؤ دلّی میں ؛ کہ شاہ باز چڑی مار کی ہے انٹی میں
نجیب چھوڑ کے شہروں کو جنگل میں خوار ؛ جنگل کو چھوڑ کے بوم آ بسے ہیں بستی میں

The nobility in Delhi though suffering from a deep seated economic crisis in the 1730s still retained great wealth during this period. Yet Hatim saw the threat from the rising commercial groups, hence the hyperbolic condemnation of the 'low born' elements in his *Shahr Ashob*,[80] belonging to 'lower professional groups such as the cobblers, vegetable venders and grocers, sweet-meat makers, jewellers and bankers. Among the *ajlaf*, the growing affluence of the bankers[81] and trading classes[82] is a matter of grave concern and receives repeated condemnation from Hatim:

Gold and Silver merchants flaunt their wealth
Golden thread weavers too live in plenty
While the jewellers play around with cash and gold.[83]

روپے اشرفی اچھالیں ہیں رات دن صرّاف ؛ مقیش و بادلے میں غرق ہیں کناری باف
ہمیشہ سونے و روپے میں کھیلتا ہے سنار

A large number of the nobles or *ashraf* whose fortunes were adversely affected, writes Nazir are too ashamed to reveal their high lineage in view of their present poverty.

Men of noble birth conceal their descent from people
In fact their behaviour enhances their dignity
There were times when so many people fed on their charity
But now it is the *Nanbai* who claims to be *ashraf*.[84]

اشرافوں نے جو اپنی یہ ذاتیں چھپائی ہیں ؛ سچ پوچھیے تو اپنی یہ شانیں بڑھائی ہیں
کہیے انھوں کی روٹیاں کس کس نے کھائی ہیں اشراف سب میں کہیے تو اب نان بائی ہیں

In a long poem entitled *Tamashagah-i-Alam* Nazir philosophically highlights the havoc that vicissitudes played on the fortunes of the people of noble descent. In this age, he laments, darkness is taken for light and light is branded as darkness.[85]

> Now a days men of noble birth work as bonded labour
> While men of low origins pretend to belong to his creed.
> Eagles and phalanx are passing a hard life
> The crocodiles are dead and the owls have taken their place
> O, Nazir, I fail to adjust myself to this strange environment.[86]

جو ہیں نجیب نسب کے وہ بندے چیلے ہیں ؂ کمینے اپنے بڑی ذات کے نویلے ہیں
جو باز شکرے ہیں پاپڑ کھڑے وہ بیلے ہیں ؂ مگر تو مر گئے الّو شکار کھیلے ہیں
غرض میں کیا کہوں دنیا بھی کیا تماشا ہے

Society according to medieval ideals assigned certain function to the *ashraf* as well as to the *ajlaf* and any deviation from the rule could mean endangering the social balance. The rising power of the traders and merchants thus posed a threat to the established functions and this was looked upon with great alarm by the literati of the period. It also symbolized the weakening of the court culture, a process, which may partly be associated with the rise of Urdu poetry and its growing popularity among cross sections of society.

Customs, Festivals and Value System

Revivalist and puritanical teachings notwithstanding, the eighteenth century was an age of eclecticism and cultural synthesis. Although Urdu poetry largely mirrors contemporary Muslim beliefs, social prejudices and predilections, it also incorporates varied aspects of cultural life commonly shared by Hindus and Muslims. The Urdu poetry of the period, perhaps more than any other single source, reflects the socio-cultural assimilation of the last two centuries. It emerged both as an instrument as well as symbol of the fruition of Indo-Islamic culture in the eighteenth century.

Mutual adoption and assimilation of Muslim and Hindu customs and beliefs such as visiting the tombs of the saints like Qutubuddin Bakhtiyarkaki, Nizamuddin Auliya and Nasiruddin Chiragh Delhi,[87] the celebration of urs of these saints as well as common celebration of various festivals formed the popular features of the religious and social life of the people. Shah Waliullah's warnings to Muslims to beware of the decline of Islamic institutions, advising them to give up the habits and customs of the *Ajam*[88] had little effect on the socio-religious practices of the period. The Shah's injunctions against adoption of Hindu dress and eating their food were considered unrealistic even by his son, Shah Abdul Aziz, who did not consider any harm in putting the dress of the Hindus for the sake of convenience and comfort.[89] A large number of common beliefs, practices and customs associated with social and religious life are reflected in the poetry of Mir, Sauda and Nazir. A number of Sauda's marsiahs though traditionally describing the tragedy of Karbala also, to a large extent, reflect the cultural traditions and beliefs common among Hindus and Muslims. For example, in the marsiah on Imam Husain, the appearance of a lion to guard his body or the satirization of Yazid by a Firangi and the latter's murder or the recitation of the Kalima by the severed head of Imam Husain[90] reflect common beliefs in the Indian context. Sauda, in fact, narrates the events of Karbala and its participation in the context of the Indian social milieu.

Several other verses of Sauda and Nazir refer to several ceremonies regarding birth and marriages common among the Muslims and Hindus. These include *telcharana, sachaq, Sehra, Barat, Bidai*[91] etc. In a long poem written on the birth of Lord Krishna, Nazir describes the occasion in the typical Indian tradition with singing of *zachcha* songs and presentation of *Neg* and *chhati* to the relatives and mother of the child.[92] Several ceremonies associated with death like *Chehlum* which was a common practice among the Hindus and Muslims and condemned by orthodox Muslim leaders continued to be celebrated by both the communities with great reverence for their dead relations.

The celebration of festivals formed one extremely popular aspect of the cultural life among all communities and classes. The festivals of Id, Holi, Diwali and Dashehra were celebrated with great fervour at the court as well as outside it. In one of his qasidas Sauda describes in detail the festivities at the court of Awadh on the occasion of Id. According to the poet, the people proceed to the court bringing costly Nazrs, the sound of music and singing can be heard from every house while one and all are immersed in merry making.[93] In such an atmosphere, Sauda concedes the rigid moral standards are thrown to the winds so much so that even the guardians of public morals, the Shaikh and the *zahid*, are seen happily enjoying the company of the wine bibbers.

> The muhtasib is seen embracing wine-bibbers
> While the zahid does not mind if a few drops fall on his clothes.[94]

معانقہ بجہاں آج مے پرستوں کی ۓ کرے ہے محتسب آکر بانبساط تمام

No one seems to care for the guardians of Shariat while the most daring among them have made a kite out of the qazi's proclamation against wine drinking.[95] The Muslims also participated with great fervour in the celebration of Hindu festivals like Holi, Diwali and Dashehra while the Hindus joined in Muslim festivities including mourning on the occasion of Muharram. Mir describes in detail the celebration of Holi in Awadh in[96] which the Nawabs themselves participated. Referring to Holi as the Noroz of Hindustan Mir writes:

> Asafuddaulah, the wazir plays Holi
> The festival of Nuroz of Hindustan
> Young and old throw colour
> Freely indulging in merry making.[97]

ہولی کھیلا آصف الدولہ وزیر ۓ رنگ صحبت سے عجب ہیں خرد و پیر

جشن نوروزِ اہلِ ہند سب ہے یہی تب محو عشرت ہیں گے اب

The nawabs of Awadh, like the later Mughal emperors, continued the tradition of Akbar's times of celebrating important Hindu festivals at the court. During the reign of emperor Shah Alam II, despite the bankruptcy of the court, the Mughal tradition of celebrating all Hindu and Muslim festivals at the court was continued. On the Dashehra day, the superintendent of the royal Karkhana displayed before the emperor furniture, elephants and horses and offered congratulations. Other festivals like Holi, Diwali and Rakhi were celebrated with great enthusiasm. Trays of traditional clay toys and sweets were brought to the emperor in the Diwan-i-Khas though money gifts never exceeded a couple of rupees.[98] The festival of Basant was also celebrated on a grand scale both at the royal court and outside it throughout north India. In Delhi people gathered in neighbouring shrines and gardens to indulge in festivities and merry making which continued for seven days.[99] All the festivals continued to be celebrated not merely at the court level but by the common masses of Hindus and Muslims. Broughton, commenting on the eclectic spirit of the age writes how the Muslims of India adopted Hindu customs to the extent of making the Muslims of India a distinct class from their brethren in other parts of the Muslim world.[100]

Muslim participation in many Hindu festivals and fairs is also reflected in Nazir's poetry who captures the enthusiasm and local colour in a number of poems written on Holi, Diwali, Rakhi, Basant and local fairs like Baldevji Ka Mela.[101] Hindu participation similarly in Muslim festivals remained a common feature of the age. The celebration of the festival of Muharram, especially in the territories of Mahadaji Sindhia, attracted the attention of contemporary observers: Mahadaji Sindhia himself dressed as faqir in the month of Muharram while many Maratha Sardars took out *tazias* on the occasion. A large number of Hindus suspended their entertainment in the month of Moharram to share the mourning with their Muslim brethren.[102] Moharram, though an occasion of frequent clashes between Shias and Sunnis also continued to be celebrated by both sects with great enthusiasm and attempts were made to maintain sectarian peace and harmony on the occasion. The Chishti saint, Shah Fakharuddin used to join the Shias in mourning in the month of Moharram, expressing grief on the martyrdom of Husain and also joined them in *fateha* prayers on the occasion.[103]

The atmosphere of religious amity and even eclecticism did not free the society of its traditional social stratification and prejudices. Among the Hindus the caste system remained dominant while the Muslim society, though theoretically upholding the principle of minimum of class distinctions could not escape the influence of caste in terms of classification into *ashraf* and *ajlaf*,[104] that is high and low born. Any attempt by the *Ajlaf* to rise above his assigned status invited deep resentment and suspicion of society an aspect repeatedly voiced by poets from Hatim to Mir, Sauda and Nazir.

Mir for example satirizes at length one Inayatullah, *alias* Kallu Hajjam, who belonging to the *ajlaf* aspired to become a poet and even managed to become a pupil of Sauda. Such a man, points out Mir, could not possibly possess the necessary talent or even commonsense to write verses, a task which he considered well beyond the capacity of a man of his background.[105] Besides it would upset the arrangement of social functions assigned to each class by society, "what will happen if society was left without cobblers, where would one find a person to mend one's shoes? And what is the need for them to become poets".[106]

> What have *ajlaf* to do with finer points of literature
> And what has poetry to do with cloth merchants and cotton cleaners'.[107]

نکتہ پردازی سے اجلافوں کو کیا ؎ شعر سے بزّازوں ندّافوں کو کیا

Mir continues the tirade against the '*hajjam*' poet, pointing out:

> Mir and Mirza may well understand each other
> But what has this barber to do with poetry.[108]

میر و مرزا حکم ہووے خرد ؎ نے کی نائی جن پہ سب کا دست رد
سمجھے مرزا میر کو مرزا کو میر ؎ نے وہ رگ زن جو نہ سمجھے سیر شیر

Mir also expresses displeasure against Sauda for having encouraged a man of such low origins to seek the company of the greatest of the poets.[109]

Among the *ashraf* the Syeds enjoyed eminence and respect in Muslim society who along with Shaikhs were "peculiar objects of respect and favour" and were entitled to gifts and charities.[110] To belong to a syed family became a symbol of social status, so much so that led many Muslims to aspire to claim syed lineage. Mir himself claimed syed descent which provoked a heated debate over the issue among contemporary *tazkirah* writers.[111] Mir himself exclaims in defence of his Syed descent:

> What if a low born refuses to call me a Syed
> My status (*sharafat*) is known to every one.[112]

رکھتی ہے میری شرافت اشتہار ؎ گو یہ ناسیّد کہے ہے کیا چمار

At an other place he writes:

None dare dispute the fact that Mir is a Syed
Only the self-styled Syeds may be an exception.[113]

منکر نہیں ہے کوئی سیادت کا میر کی ؛ ذاتِ مقدس ان کی یہی ذات ہو تو ہو

The Islamic social consciousness thus remained strongly under the influence of 'caste psychology' although attempts by lower social groups to attain respectability through upward movement are clearly discernible in contemporary poetry and literature, hence the great contempt and ridicule is showered on such aspirants. The following verse of Nazir seems to capture the contemporary social divisions as well as the ultimate futility of the same:

There were many men, boasting to be called Shaikhs and Pathans
All of a sudden, the death knell sounded
And swept away the Syed, Shaikhs and Mughals
Their caste, dynasty or noble birth
Could not escape clutches of death.[114]

کہتے تھے کتنے ہم تو ہیں ذات میں کلاں جی ؛ ہم شیخ ہم مغل ہیں ہم ہیں پٹھان ہاں جی
جس دم قضا پکاری اب اٹھ چلو میاں جی ؛ پھر شیخ جی نہ سید مرزا رہے نہ خاں جی
ذات و حسب نسب کا جو ہر ہوا تو پھر کیا

The traditional value system the attitude towards women and the concept of love finds free expression in the poetry of the age. The masnavi and the ghazal portray not merely the romantic tales, the lovers meeting or separation but also reveal contemporary values and social attitudes. The traditional role of women as mother, sister or wife is well portrayed in Sauda's marsiahs which capture the atmosphere of Indian homes in a vivid style.[115] The prevailing social attitudes towards women remained conservative in matters of marriage or family relationships yet an occasional voice of resentment arose in society such as a demand for a high *mehr* money at the time of marriage[116] or against other social customs unfair to women. Sauda's satire on one old Shaikh who married a girl of his daughter's age is a clear condemnation of such a practice. The old Shaikh is made a subject of great ridicule at the hands of society in general:

The Shaikh appears to be bent upon heaping infamy on his head

As if he was under God's curse to be put to disgrace
He married a minor girl of twelve
And brought the bride home with great pomp and show.[117]

القصہ شیخ جی کی جو حرمت خدا گنوائے ۔ منھ کو کلنک اپنے لگاتے ہیں شیخ جی
بارہ برس کی چھوکری باجن بجاتے لائے

The concept of love and marriage remained conservative, the two were considered entirely separate matters. Love affairs were socially acceptable only so long as they were confined to courtesans while any involvement of respectable women seemed to endanger all social norms, and brought great shame to the families involved. This also accounts for the popularity of 'courtesans' culture during the eighteenth century as it allowed free and uninhibited mixing of men and women and lovers without social condemnation. Thus Nazir, in one of his poems gives a most uninhibited description of the beauty, dress, ornaments and ways of a well known prostitute of Agra.[118] This style of poetry devoted to the description of the physical charms, dress, ornaments of the courtesans became very popular in Lucknow, where there was such abundance of dancing girls and courtesans that no street was considered free from them.[119]

Mir in one of his masnavis *Mamlaat-i-Ishq*,[120] tells the tragic story of his love affair with a girl who was a relative and probably married, with great frankness. Mir's affair incited the wrath of his family who disapproved his behaviour and their persecution drove him into temporary madness, an experience described by him in another masnavi entitled *Khab-o-Khayal*.[121] Mir's affair went against established social norms hence was bound to end in frustration and tragedy. Mir therefore advises men to avoid the path of love:

Blessed are those not affected by love
This affliction neither spares the lover nor the beloved.[122]

محبت نہ ہو کاش مخلوق کو ۔ نہ چھوڑے یہ عاشق نہ معشوق کو

Love in spite of its condemnation transcends, according to Mir, all social and religious barriers. In his poem 'on love' the beloved is a young Hindu married woman and the lover is an Afghan youth. In the *mornama* the lover is a peacock who falls in love with a beautiful queen while in *Shola-i-Ishq*, 'The fire of love', the lovers are husband and wife; a situation rather unusual in the eighteenth century life and literature alike.[123] Mir's romantic masnavis and verses tell the tale of lovers in simple verse who face with dignity and courage what they know to be an inevitable fate. When even the lovers of the great Persian and Arabics legends, Farhad and Qais, had not fared any better, Mir could hardly expect a better fate. The path of love could only bring sorrow, separation from the beloved and even a tragic end of the life of the lovers:

> The crucial test of true love is
> The lover lays down his life cheerfully in the path of love.[124]

محبت کی رہ میں یہ پہلا ہے کام ؎ کہ سر سے گذر جائیے شاد کام

In other verses Mir elaborates on the theme of tragic love:

> So many youthful souls laid down their lives at the altar of love
> And quite a number of families were ruined
> There were others who fell victim to love
> Who smeared their faces with ash and became jogis.[125]

جواں کیسے کیسے موئے عشق میں ؎ بہت گھر خرابے ہوئے عشق میں
بہت عشق میں لوگ روگی ہوئے ؎ بہت خاک مل منہ پہ جوگی ہوئے

Or

> O Mir, Love is a heavy stone
> How a weakling like you can lift it?[126]

عشق اک میر بھاری پتھر ہے ؎ کب یہ تجھ ناتواں سے اٹھتا ہے

Sauda expresses similar sentiments for the beloved:

> What has driven Sauda to such extremity?
> One fails to detect anything extraordinary in her to justify his condition.[127]

سودا جو تیرا حال ہے اتنا تو نہیں وہ ؎ کیا جانیے تو نے اسے کس آن میں دیکھا

The proud and assertive nature of the beloved in Urdu poetry well contrasts with the otherwise submissive life of a woman marked by life long subordination to the authority of the father, husband or son.

A man may die but she will never care
O God, how proud is my beloved.[128]

حضرت سے اس کی جانا کہاں ہے ؛ اب مر رہے گا یاں بندۂ درگاہ

The cultural scene of the eighteenth century, despite the orthodox ideal of an austere and God fearing society following strictly the rules of the Shariat, followed a predominantly liberal and eclectic culture. Although towards the end of the eighteenth century, the ideas of the Wahabi leader Abdul Wahab (1763-1787) began to reach India, they had little impact on contemporary socio-religious and cultural life. Even Shah Abdul Aziz disagreed with the puritancial teachings of the Wahabi leader which totally prohibited *urs* and visiting of tombs[129] as *shirk* (Polytheism) which by the eighteenth century had a socio-cultural character commonly shared by the Hindus and Muslims. Again, the affluent style of living wearing of rich clothes, jewellery, eating good food etc. censured by puritanical leaders, remained the most popular mode of living among the affluent. Certain forms of entertainment such as singing, dancing, hunting, pigeon flying, cock fights etc., condemned by the orthodoxy, remained the popular means of entertainment among all classes and sections of society.

NOTES

1. Mir, *Kulliyat*, I, p. 350.
2. C.A. Bayly, 'Delhi and other cities of North India during the 'twilight', in R.E. Frykenberg, *op. cit.*, p. 229.
3. J.N. Sarkar, *Fall of the Mughal Empire*, Volume III, p. 279.
4. Tapan Ray Chaudhury, *The Cambridge Economic History of India*, Volume II, p. 8.
5. Mir, *Kulliyat*, Volume I, p. 319.
6. *Ibid.*, p. 707.
7. Sauda, *Kulliyat*, II, pp. 264-65.
8. *Ibid.*, p. 265.
9. *Ibid.*
10. *Ibid.*
11. *Ibid.*

12. *Ibid.*, p. 266.
13. Mir Taqi Mir, *Kulliyat*, I, p. 64.
14. Hatim, *Diwanzada*, p. 120.
15. Mir Dard, *Diwan*, p. 33.
16. *Ibid.*
17. Muhammad Husain Azad, *Ab-i-Hayat*, p. 150.
18. *Tarikh-i-Alamgir Sani*, 87a-88a, *Delhi Chronicle*, quoted J.N. Sarkar, *Fall of the Mughal Empire*, II, pp. 60-62.
19. Mir, *Mir Ki Ap Biti*, pp. 137-138.
20. Hatim, *Diwanzada*, *Shah Hatim Aur Unka Kalam*, Wr. 1182, p.309.
21. T. Twining, *Travels*, p. 263.
22. Sauda, *Kulliyat*, II, p. 266.
23. Mir, *Kulliyat*, II, pp. 107-117.
24. *Ibid.*, p.108.
25. *Ibid.*, p. 117.
26. *Ibid.*, pp. 110-11, 113-114.
27. *Ibid.*, pp. 114-115.
28. *Ibid.*
29. *Ibid.*, p. 112.
30. Ibid.
31. Ibid.
32. *Ibid.*
33. *Ibid.*, p. 112.
34. T. Twining, *Travels*, pp. 269-270.
35. W. Hodges, *Travels in India in the Years 1780, 1781, 1782, 1783*, London, 1793, p. 132.
36. *Ibid.*, p., 111.
37. Nazir, *Kulliyat*, p. 336; J.N. Sarkar, *Delhi Affairs*, pp. 113, 117-118, 125.
38. *Ibid.*, p. 173.
39. Mir, *Mir-Ki Ap Biti*, pp. 142-143; W. Hodges, *Travels*, pp. 114-115, 132; J.N. Sarkar, *Delhi Affairs*, p. 165.
40. Nazir, *Kulliyat*, pp. 338-339.
41. *Ibid.*, Although a large number of professional groups suffered hardships with the decline of the nobles, the number mentioned by Nazir need not be taken literally as 36 *Paunis* or professions is the traditional number mentioned in the medieval literature. See Savitri Chandra, *Social Life and concepts in Medieval Hindi Bhakti poetry*, pp. 32-33.
42. *Ibid.*
43. *Ibid.*, p. 339.
44. C.A. Bayly, *Rulers, Townsmen and Bazaars*, pp. 79-80.
45. H. Naqvi, *Urban Centres*, pp. 39-40, 49-53.
46. Murtaza Husain, Translation, W. Irvine, 'Ahmad Shah Abdali and the Indian Wazir Imadulmulk' in *Indian Antiquary*, p. 13.
47. *Calendar of Persian correspondence*, V, 1079; A. Das Gupta, in D.S. Richards edited, *op. cit.*, p. 184.
48. Ghulam Muhammad Khan, *Travels*, 37b, quoted, H.K. Naqvi, *op. cit.*, p. 14; S. Nurul Hasan, 'The Morphology of a Medieval Indian city: A case study of Shahjahanabad in the 18th and early 19th century'. *Indian History Congress*, Kurukshetra, 1982.
49. Mir, *Kulliyat*, I, p. 235.
50. Sauda, *Kulliyat*, I, p. 279.
51. *Ibid.*

52. *Tarikh-i-Alamgir Sani*, 148, *Delhi Chronicle*, quoted, J.N. Sarkar, *Fall of the Mughal Empire*, Volume III, pp. 107-108.

53. Faulad Khan was a descendant of Habsh Khan (real name Sidi Miftah) who lived in the reign of Shahjahan and Aurangzeb. Sidi Miftah was an Abyssinian by extract and originally a slave of Nizam Shahi Kings of Ahmadnager who later joined service of Shahjahan and was given the title of Habsh Khan, raised to the rank of 3000 Zat and 1,500 Sawar – See Shah Nawaz Khan, *Maasirul Umara*, Volume, I, pp. 594-596.

54. Sauda, *Kulliyat*, I, p. 282.

55. *Ibid.*

56. J.N. Sarkar, *Fall of the Mughal Empire*, Volume II, pp. 18-22.

57. Sauda, *Kulliyat*, I, p. 279.

58. *Ibid.*, p. 281.

59. *Ibid.*, P. 226.

60. Dargah Quli Khan, *Muraqqa-i-Delhi.*

61. T. Twining, *Travels*, p. 242.

62. *Ibid.*

63. Mir, *Kulliyat*, I, p. 141.

64. T. Twining, *Travels*, pp. 275, 278, 279-280; Broughton, *Letters from a Mahratta camp*, pp. 72-73, 214. But the ceremony and quality of Khilat did not match Mughal polish or quality, P. Spear, *Twilight of the Mughals*, pp. 81-83.

65. Sauda, *Kulliyat*, I, pp. 216-217.

66. *Ibid*, pp. 172-181.

67. *Ibid.*, pp. 184-194.

68. *Ibid.*, p. 185.

69. W. Irvine, 'Ahmad Shah Abdali and the Indian Wazir Imadulmulk', *Indian Antiquary*, p. 45.

70. Mir, *Kulliyat*, II, pp. 58-61, 161-170.

71. *Ibid.*, I, p. 597.

72. Mir, *Mir Ki Ap Biti*, p. 183.

73. Dargah Quli Khan, *Muraqqa-i-Dehli*, p. 201.

74. Sauda, *Kulliyat*, I, p. 196.

75. Mir, *Kulliyat*, II, pp. 419.

76. Shah Waliullah, *Maktubat*, p. 43; W. Hodges, *Travels*, pp. 21-22; Dargah Quli Khan, *Muraqqa-i-Dehli*, pp. 154-155.

77. Hatim, *Diwan-i-Qadim*, pp. 274-275.

78. Sauda, *Kulliyat*, II, pp. 258-260.

79. Hatim, *Diwan-i-Qadim*, p. 275.

80. *Ibid.*, pp. 274-275.

81. *Ibid.*, p. 274.

82. *Ibid.*

83. *Ibid.*, p. 274.

84. Nazir, *Kulliyat*, p. 202.

85. *Ibid.*, p. 151.

86. *Ibid.*, pp. 150.

87. Dargah Quli Khan, *Muraqqa-i-Dehli*, pp. 120-121, 123.

88. Shah Waliullah, *Wasiyat Nama*, p. 11, *Maktubat*, edited K.A. Nazimi, p. 96.

89. Shah Abdul Aziz, *Fatwa-i-Shah Abdul Aziz*, Delhi, 1893, Vol. I, p.110.

90. Sauda, *Kulliyat*, II, pp. 315.

91. Sauda, *Kulliyat*, II, pp. 312, 314, 332, 368.

92. Sauda, *Kulliyat*, I, pp. 194-95 Nazir, *Kulliyat*, pp. 60, 100-101, 103.

93. Sauda, *Kulliyat*, I, p. 196.
94. *Ibid.*
95. *Ibid.*
96. Mir, *Kulliyat*, II, pp. 163-164, 168-170.
97. *Ibid.*, p. 168.
98. Tekchand, *Roznamcha-i-Shah Alam*, 495b, 394b, 527a, f, 222a, quoted, S.A.A. Rizvi, *Shah Abdul Aziz*, p. 47.
99. Dargah Quli Khan, *Muraqqa-i-Dehli*, pp. 147-149.
100. J.D. Broughton, *Letters from a Mahratta Camp*, p. 205.
101. Nazir, *Kulliyat*, pp. 216-245.
102. T.D. Broughton, *Letters from a Mahratta Camp*, pp. 51-52.
103. Qazi Bashiruddin, *Malfuzat-i-Shah Abdul Aziz*, p. 81, quoted, K.A. Nizami, *Mashaikh*, p. 221.
104. J.A. Malcolm, *Memoir of central India*, London, 1832, Vol. II, pp.110-111; Martin Montgomery (ed.). *Antiquities Topography, Statistics of Eastern India*, by F.H. Buchanan, London, 1837, Vol. I, pp. 145-146; Also see Imtiaz Ahmad, 'The Ashraf-Ajlaf dichotomy in Muslim Social Structure' in *Economic and Social History Review*, 1966, Vol. III, No. 3, p. 273-74.
105. Mir, *Kulliyat*, II, p. 142.
106. *Ibid.*
107. *Ibid.*
108. *Ibid.*, p. 149.
109. *Ibid.*
110. *Mrs Meer Hasan Ali*, *op. cit.*, Volume I, pp. 6-7.
111. See Chapter, II, pp. 40-41.
112. Mir, *Kulliyat*, II, p. 134.
113. *Ibid.*, I, p. 691.
114. Nazir, *Kulliyat*, p. 161.
115. Sauda, *Kulliyat* II, pp. 332-33, 337-38.
116. Shah Waliullah, *Wasiyat Nama*, 11-12, advocated a low rate of *mehr* in accordance to Shariat but favoured widow remarriage, condemning Hindu practice in not allowing the same.
117. Sauda, *Kulliyat*, II, p. 243.
118. Makhmoor Akbarabadi, *Rooh-i-Nazir*, pp. 336-339.
119. Abdul Halim Sharar, *Guzashta Lucknow*, p. 51.
120. Mir, *Kulliyat*, II, pp. 50-62.
121. *Ibid.*, pp. 86-92.
122. *Ibid.*, II, p. 36.
123. Ralph Russell, Khurshidul Islam, *Three Mughal Poets*, London, 1969, p.103.
124. Mir, *Kulliyat*, II, p. 82.
125. *Ibid.*, p. 93.
126. *Ibid.*, I, p. 192.
127. Sauda, *Kulliyat*, I, p. 409.
128. Mir, *Kulliyat*, I, p. 173.
129. Shah Abdul Aziz, *Fatwa-i-Shah Abdul Aziz*, Vol. I, p. 94.

7

CONCLUSION

The historical content of the Urdu poetry of the second half of the eighteenth century covers some major aspects of society and politics of the period. These include the nature of contemporary politics, the decline of Mughal imperial authority and its impact on the institutions of monarchy, the nobility as well as on the prevailing socio-political attitudes towards these institutions. The poetry of the age also gave voice to such concepts as mysticism, eclecticism, religious toleration and humanism which provided a distinctive character to the culture of the eighteenth century. The picture of society that emerges from the poetry of Hatim, Sauda, Mir, Dard and Nazir, though necessarily circumscribed by the social background and outlook of the poets, highlights the variegated facets of the eighteenth century life in an age of transition, from the glitter and pomp of the reign of Muhammad Shah to the austerity and poverty of the court of Shah Alam II. While touching on the rise of the 'new' court culture in Lucknow, it provides a vivid account of life comparatively free of court influences in Delhi, Agra and its environs.

As regards the problem of distintegration of the Mughal empire, Sauda's account, more than any other poets', highlights some of the complex problems facing the empire including the crisis of Mansabdari and Jagirdari systems, the resulting bankruptcy of the central government the administrative breakdown and the adverse effects of the predatory activities of the Marathas, Jats and Sikhs on the stability of the empire. His account of the political role of the nobles of Delhi, their disloyalty, corruption and indifference to the fate of the empire is extremely realistic. Contrary to the viewpoint of the theologians, the literati did not see the armed conflict between different factions within India in religious terms but from a broader perspective of administrative decline. The poets, however, failed to establish a causal link between political and economic crises of the empire and the self aggrandizement of the nobles and other centrifugal tendencies.

The nature of the eulogization of the contemporary Mughal emperors like Alamgir II and Shah Alam II, despite their political weakness, economic bankruptcy and frequent instances of derogation which a poet like Zatalli had dared to highlight (which cost him his life) long before Sauda and Mir wrote their eulogies, needs to be studied in the broader perspective of the survival of the idea of royal legitimacy as embodied in Mughal dynastic rule in the eighteenth century. Both Sauda and Mir shower praise on the monarchical system of government especially its paternal role, which alone, according to medieval concepts was capable of ensuring conditions of peace, prosperity and security of the governed. The poets lament at the decline of the authority of the kings but nowhere criticize the institution itself, but only the weaknesses that characterized the monarchy during the period.

The contemporary nobility remains the subject of both eulogization as well as criticism by the poets. As the nobility was considered indispensable in the proper functioning of the monarchical system of government, Sauda and Mir lay great emphasis on the cultivation of ideal qualities in the nobles such as valour, sense of justice and generosity. The poets view the decline of the nobles, primarily in terms of that section of the Mughal nobles which had become economically bankrupt and politically weak, and disloyal to the empire, hence are subjected to great satirization by Sauda. Both the poets, however, do not hesitate from eulogizing some of the nobles who were successful in carving out their own independent principalities, as in the case of the nawabs of Awadh. This obvious dichotomy in the poets' attitude to a large extent explains the contemporary political attitude of accepting the fate accompli vis-a-vis the empire. The political elites as well as the intellectuals show little keenness in the revival of Mughal dynastic rule; showing preference for those provincial or local rulers who being indifferent to the Mughal cause, had used its halo to fulfil their political ambitions and established conditions of peace and security in their respective states.

The eighteenth century Urdu poetry served as an effective and powerful instrument in the defusion of the prevailing ideals of mysticism, liberalism and humanism. Poets like Mir Dard, Mir and Hatim made a significant contribution to writings on sufistic themes which largely portrayed the contemporary philosophy of life. Sufistic concepts such as belief in the vanity of life, renunciation, asceticism and unworldliness, attained great popularity in the eighteenth century. This "pessimism" written large on the contemporary thought became a dominant feature of the poetry written in Delhi where fear and insecurity of life constantly threatened the populace. Mir's first diwan, for example, is full of grief stricken contemplation regarding the futility of existence, happiness is seen but as a fleeting moment in the strain of living while life itself is looked upon as a burden one is compelled to carry in preparation for death.

> It is advisable to have some good deeds to one's credit
> For a large number of caravans are often ready for departure.[1]

اندیشہ زادِ راہ کا رکھئے تو ہے مناسب ؛ چلنے کو یاں سے اکثر تیار قافلے ہیں

Death levels all differences between the great and the mean and the lowly, hence the utter futility of life in the face of death:

> Be they kings or beggers, all will go empty handed
> Neither kings would take their crowns and thrones
> Nor the beggers their cap and mat.[2]

اور جس وقت بادشاہ و گدا ؛ اس جہاں سے کریں گے عزم سفر
نہ تو لے تاج و تخت جاوے گا ؛ کلہ و بوریا نہیں لے کر

The transitory nature of existence is repeatedly stressed, every one from the king to the begger has ultimately to go to dust. The following verses of Mir, for instance, admonish man against undue pride warning that ultimately death comes one day to level all men to dust:

> Yesterday, I happened to trample over a skull,
> It was totally crushed to dust,
> The skull appeared to be admonishing me in mute language
> Against vanity and conciet
> Remembering that it too once formed part of a proud head.[3]

کل پاؤں ایک کاسۂ سر پر جو آ گیا ؛ یک سر وہ استخوان شکستوں سے چور تھا
کہنے لگا کہ دیکھ کے چل راہ بے خبر ؛ میں بھی کبھو کسو کا سر پُر غرور تھا

A similar philosophical attitude is adopted by Nazir in the midst of themes otherwise vibrating with life:

> If one becomes a king and extends his rule over vast territories, so what?
> If the sound of trumpets rent the air for a couple of days, so what?
> If the fame of his greatness spread far and wide, so what?
> Or if he turned a recluse with a coloured robe, so what?[4]

گر بادشہ ہو کر عمل ملکوں ہوا تو کیا ہوا ؎ دو دن کا نرسنگا بجا بھوں بھوں ہوا تو کیا ہوا
غل شور ملک و مال کا کوسوں ہوا تو کیا ہوا ؎ یا ہو فقیر آزاد کے رنگوں ہوا تو کیا ہوا

All wordly goods, including wealth and fame, continues Nazir, do not come to one's rescue, once the caravans begin to move away.[5] As regards the present, one can hope for little, it is futile to worry about future for one would face it when it arrives, if spared by death.[6] Regarding happiness, it may exist, but at least Mir has little experience of it himself.[7] In another verse Mir enquires about the duration of happiness which lasts just as long as the fragrance of a flower.

> Deep thinking led Mir to the conclusion
> That happy span of life was like the sweet fragrance of a flower.[8]

خوب دریافت جو کیا ہم نے ؎ وقت خوش میرؔ نکہتِ گل تھا

The devastation and ruin which followed the fall of Delhi thus strengthened the mystic ideals of the unreality of worldly splendour and contempt for material wealth which found expression in the elegiac style of poetry written in Delhi. Such deep pessimism and mysticism is absent in poetry written outside Delhi territories including Agra where conditions of comparative peace and security prevailed. In case of Lucknow the ruling classes relieved from the duties of administration and responsibility gave themselves up to pleasure and debauchery. Poetry lacking in depth and sentiment, all polish, wit and glitter, presented a faithful reflection of life of Lucknow which could have little use for ideas of mysticism and asceticism.

Mysticism, however, remained the most popular aspect of religious and intellectual life of the period. The religious atmosphere was marked by a spirit of toleration and eclecticism which found free expression in the Urdu ghazal of the times. The prevailing spirit of religious amity and goodwill was not violated by the tyranny of the ecclesiastical classes though orthodox and puritanical movements raised their heads in the second half of the eighteenth century. The Mughal emperors and the independent rulers, far from acting as allies of religious revivalism lent encouragement and support to the eclectic and liberal religious outlook of the age.

The collapse of the Mughal authority and the ruin of Delhi in the years 1739 to 1760, did not imply a total destruction of the old society and culture. Mir and Sauda, who lament the fate of Delhi also eulogize and praise the peace, security and prosperity as well as patronage of men of talent, in the new states that rose on the ruins of the empire. Their poetry in fact reflect both continuity and change in the political, socio-economic and cultural life of the age. The poets' grief at the decline of the nobles of Delhi by no means implied a total cessation of social and economic activity in the capital. With the decline of old patrons, many wealthy men of the city including the Maratha leaders emerged as new patrons in the 1770s and 1780s. Among the new social groups which rose to prominence during this period were a large number of Jain and Khatri trading communities who took keen interest in building activity, constructing temples, houses and Katras in Shahjahanabad. At the cultural level the mystique of the Mughal court culture still held sway not only over the Maratha rulers of Delhi but also enamoured the British, who replaced them in 1803.

Economically, though Delhi suffered extreme hardships, the capital slowly recovered the losses. Taking advantage of the plight of the majority of the nobles, certain powerful economic groups such as bankers, money-lenders and petty traders rose to rapid prominence to make quick profits in the given situation. The rise of these groups forms the subject of satirization by Hatim who notes their rise to power with extreme contempt and dismay. Even Nazir "the poet of the people" expresses similar regret at the rise of these 'low born' at the cost of 'great and the noble' in the city of Agra.

A subtle change is also discernible in the values and social attitudes as well as life style of the nobles in view of the economic hardships suffered by them in Delhi which does not find the approval of Sauda and Mir. In Awadh where conditions of peace and plenty prevailed, a new set of cultural norms and life style emerged which claimed superiority over Delhi's language and cultural norms, even in matters of dress and food.[9] This 'new society' earned the dislike of the poets of Delhi particularly Mir who found himself in a different world altogether and which in turn did not seem to care for Mir's approval.

> You Easterners, why do you make fun of me,
> And ask about my homeland,
> There was a city, famous and renowned
> where the select few of the age lived,
> Delhi is the name, fairest among fair,
> Fate looted and destroyed it
> And to that desolate city I belong.[10]

کیا بود و باش پوچھو ہو پورب کے ساکنو ؎ ہم کو غریب جان کے ہنس ہنس پکار کے
دلّی جو ایک شہر تھا عالم میں انتخاب ؎ رہتے تھے منتخب ہی جہاں روزگار کے
اس کو فلک نے لوٹ کے ویران کر دیا ؎ ہم رہنے والے ہیں اسی اجڑے دیار کے

NOTES

1. Mir, *Kulliyat*, I, p. 367.
2. Sauda, *Kulliyat*, II, p. 159.
3. Mir, *Kulliyat*, I, p. 19.
4. Nazir, *Kulliyat*, p. 154.
5. *Ibid.*, p. 122.
6. Mir, *Kulliyat*, I, p. 363.
7. *Ibid.*, p. 185.
8. *Ibid.*, p. 26.
9. Syed Insha, *Dariya-i-Latafat*, pp. 67-68, 104-105, 107-108, 113.
10. Muhammad Husain Azad, *Ab-i-Hayat*, p. 206.

BIBLIOGRAPHY

PRIMARY SOURCES

Poetical Works

Dard, Khwajah Mir, *Diwan-i-Dard*, New Delhi, 1982.

Hatim, Shaikh Zahuruddin, *Diwanzada*, (ed.), Ghulam Husain Zufiqar, Lahore, 1975.

Hatim, *Diwan-i-Qadim*, (ed.), Maulvi Abdul Haq, Delhi, 1977.

Mir Taqi Mir, *Kulliyat-i-Mir*, 2 Volumes, Allahabad, 1972.

Mir Taqi Mir, *Kulliyat-i-Mir*, (ed.), Abdul Bari Asi, Lucknow, 1941.

Nazir Akbarabadi, *Kulliyat-i-Nazir*, Allahabad, 1976.

Sauda, Mirza Muhammad Rafi, *Kulliyat-i-Sauda*, 2 Volumes, Allahabad, 1972.

Sauda, Mirza Muhammad Rafi, *Kulliyat-i-Sauda*, 2 Volumes, Lucknow, 1932.

Tazkirah, Biography and Literary Works

Ali, Shah Ghulam, *Maqamat-i-Mazhari*, Delhi, 1891.

Azad, Muhammad Husain, *Ab-i-Hayat*, Allahabad, 1980.

Azfari, Muhammad Zahiruddin, *Waqiat-i-Azfari*, Translation, A. Sattar, Madras, 1937.

Aziz, Shah Abdul, *Fatwa-i-Shah Abdul Aziz*, Delhi, 1893.

Baharaichi, Maulvi Naimullah, *Mamlat-i-Mazhariyya*, Kanpur, 1275 H.

Bashiruddin, Qazi Muhammad, *Malfuzat-i-Shah Abdul Aziz*, Meerut.

Firaq, Nasir, *Maikhana-i-Dard*, Delhi, 1925.

Gardizi, Fateh Ali Husain, *Tazkirah-i-Rekhta Goyan*, Aurangabad, 1933.

Hamid Aurangabadi, Khwajah Khań, *Tazkirah Gulshan-i-Guftar*, Lucknow, 1963.

Hasan, Mir, *Tazkirah-i-Shuara-i-Urdu*, Aligarh, 1922.

Hindi, Bhagwandas, *Safina-i-Hindi*, Patna, 1958.

Insha, Syed Insha Allahkhan, *Dariya-i-Latafat*, Translated by Pandit Brij Mohan Kaifi, Aurangabad, 1935.

Jan-i-Janan, Mirza Mazhar, *Khutoot*, Translated and (ed.), Khaliq Anjum, Delhi, 1962.

Khan, Dargah Quli, *Muraqqa-i-Dehli*, Urdu translation Nurul Hasan Ansari, Delhi, 1982.

Lutf, Mirza Ali, *Gulshan-i-Hind*, Lahore, 1906.

Mir, Taqi Mir, *Zikr-i-Mir*, Urdu translation, Nisar Ahmad Faruqi as *Mir ki Ap Biti*, Delhi, 1957.

Mir, Taqi Mir, *Nikatush Shuara*, Delhi, 1972.

Mir Dard, *Ilmul Kitab*, Delhi, 1892.

Mir Dard, *Risail-i-Araba-i-Dard*, Bhopal.

Mushafi, Ghulam Hamdani, *Tazkirah-i-Hindi*, Delhi, 1933.

Mushafi, Ghulam Hamdani, *Aqd-i-Suraiya*, Urdu translation, Alaur Rehman, Patna, 1968.

Nasir, Saadat Khan, *Tazkirah-i-Khushmarka-i-Zeba*, 2 Volumes, Lahore, 1970.

Qasim, Hakim Qudratullah, *Majmua-i-Naghz*, 2 Volumes, Delhi, 1973.

Qayam, Qayamuddin, *Makhzan-i-Nikat*, Aurangabad, 1929.

Rangin, Saadat Khan, *Majalis-i-Rangin*, (ed.), Syed Masud Hasan Rizvi, Lucknow, 1929.

Shafiq, Laxmi Narayan, *Chamanistan-i-Shuara*, Aurangabad, 1929.

Shahwaliullah, *Hujjatullah Baligha*, Urdu translation, Abdul Haq Haqqam, Karachi.

Shahwaliullah, *Wasiyat Nama*, Urdu translation by Syed Zahiruddin, Delhi, 1899.

Shahwaliullah, *Fayuzul Harmayn*, Urdu translation, Syed Zahiruddin Ahmad, Delhi.

Shahwaliullah, *Maktubat*, edited, K.A. Nizami, Aligarh, 1950.

Sharar, Abdul Halim, *Guzashta Lucknow*, New Delhi, 1971.

Shauq, Qudratullah, *Tazkirah-i-Tabqat-i-Shuara*, Lahore, 1968.

Shefta, Muhammad Mustafa Khan, *Gulshan-i-Bekhar*, Karachi, 1963.

Historical Works

Abdul Karim, Khwajah, *Bayan-i-Waqai*, (ed.), K.B. Nasim, Lahore, 1970.

Abul Fazl, *Ain-i-Akbari*, Translation, Blochmann, New Delhi, 1965.

Anonymous, *Tarikh-i-Alamgir Sani*, B.M. MS No. 1749. J.N. Sarkar's Rotograph copy, Rieu III, 942.

Anonymous, *Delhi Chronicle* MS., Described by J.N. Sarkar in IHRC, Vol. II, 1921.

Anonymous, *Tarikh-i-Ahmad Shahi*, B.M. MS or 2005. J.N. Sarkar Rotograph copy, Rieu III, 941.

Ashub, Muhammad Bakhsh, *Tarikh-i-Shahadat-i-Farrukhsiyar wa Julus-i-Muhammad Shahi*, B.M., M.S. Rieu III, Rotograph, Aligarh.

Azad, Ghulam Ali Bilgrami, *Khizan-i-Amira*, Kanpur, 1900.

Bakhsh, Muhammad Faiz, *Tarikh-i-Farah Bakhsh*, Translation by W. Hoey, *Memoirs of Delhi and Faizabad*, 2 Volumes, Allahabad, 1889.

Firaqi, Kanwar Prem Kishore, *Waqai-Alamshahi*, Rampur, 1949.

Ghani, Najmul, *Tarikh-i-Awadh*, 2 Vols., Lucknow, 1919.

Husain, Ghulam, *Siyarul Mutakherin*, Urdu translation, Gokul Prasad, Lucknow, 1874.

Husain, Murtaza, *Hadiqatul Aqalim*, Lucknow, 1879.

Khafi Khan, Muhammad Hashim, *Muntakhabul Lubab*, Calcutta, 1874.

Khan, Ghulam, Ali, *Shah Alam Nama*, MS. J.N. Sarkar's copy.

Khan, Muhammad Ali, *Tarikh-i-Muzaffari*, Aligarh MS.

Khan, Mustajab, *Gulistan-i-Rehmat*, Translated C. Elliot, The Life of Hafizoolmoolk, London, 1831.

Khan, Shah Nawaz, *Maasirul Umara*, 2 Volumes, English Translation by H. Beveredge and Beni Prasad, Patna, 1979.

Khan, Shakir, *Tarikh-i-Shakir Khani*, BM, MS Rieu I, 279 B Add. 6585.

Munalal, *Tarikh-i-Shah Alam*, Oriental Public Library, Patna.

Shafiwarid Tehrani, *Mirat-i-waridat*, Bankipur, VII.

Tekchand, *Roznamcha-i-Shah Alam*, M.S. Khuda Bakhsh Library, Patna, VII, 620.

European Accounts

Broughton, T.D., *Letters from a Mahratta camp during the year 1809*, Westminster.

Buchanan, Hamilton, *The History Antiquities, Topography and Statistics of Eastern India*, (ed.), Montgomery Martin, 3 Volumes, London, 1837.

Crooke, William, edited, *Mrs. Meer Hasan Ali's Observations on the Mussulmans of India*, Delhi, 1973.

Forster, George, *A Journey from Bengal to England through the Northern parts of India, Kashmir, Afghanistan and Persia*, London, 1798.

Heber, Bishop Reginald, *Narrative of a Journey through the upper Provinces of India*, 2 Volumes, 1828.

Hodges, W., *Travels in India in the years 1780, 1781, 1782, 1783*, London, 1793.

Malcolm, Sir, J.A., *Memoir of Central India*, 2 Volumes, London, 1832.

Mill, James and Wilson, H.H., *History of British India*, 10 Volumes, 1858.

Orme, R. *Historical, Fragments of the Mogul Empire*, London, MOCCV.

Polier, A.L.H., *Shah Alam II and his court: A narrative of the transactions at the court of Dehly form the year 1771*, (ed.), P.C. Gupta, Calcutta, 1947.

Stavorinus, J.S., *Voyage to the East Indies*, London, 1798.

Tenant, William, *Indian Recreations consisting chiefly of strictures on the domestic and rural economy of the Mohammadans and Hindoos*, London, 1802.

Twining, Thomas, *Travels in India a hundred years Ago*, (ed.), Rev. H.C. William, London, 1893.

Ward, Rev., W. *View of the History Literature and Religion of the Hindoos*, London 1817.

Published Records and Documents and Gazetteers

Atkinson, E., *Statistical, Descriptive and Historical Account of North-west Province of India*, Allahabad, 1875.

Calendar of Persian Correspondence, Imperial Records department, III, Calcutta, 1919, VI, Delhi, 1938.

English Records of Maratha History, Poona Residency Correspondence, Vol. I, Mahadaji Sindhia and Northern Affairs 1785-1794, Tr. J.N. Sarkar, Bombay, 1936.

Nevill, H.R., *District Gazetteers of the United Provinces*, Allahabad, 1919.

Persian Records of Maratha History, (ed.), P.M. Joshi, Vol. I, Delhi Affairs 1761-1788, Tr. J.N. Sarkar, Bombay, 1953.

Proceedings of Indian Historical Records Commission, 1921, 1940.

Selections from the Peshwa's daftar, (ed.), G.S. Sardesai XXI, XXVII.

Thorntorn, Edward, A. *Gazetteer of the Territories of the East India Company and of the Native States on the Continent of India*, London, 1854.

SECONDARY SOURCES

Urdu

Abdullah, Syed, *Mubahis, Tahqiqi aur Tanqidi Muzamin*, Lahore, 1965.
Abdullah, Syed, *Naqd-i-Mir*, Lahore, 1958.
Ah, Safdar, *Mir Aur Miryat*, Bombay, 1972.
Ahmad, Naeem, *Shehr Ashob Ka Tahqiqi Mutala*, Aligarh, 1979.
Akhtar, Waheed, *Khwajah Mir Dard, Tasawwuf Aur Shairi*, Aligarh, 1971.
Anjum, Khaliq, *Mirza Rafi Sauda*, Aligarh, 1968.
Chand, Shaikh, *Sauda*, Aurangabad, 1936.
Faruqi, Khwaja Ahmad, *Mir Taqi Mir, Hayat Aur Shairi*, Aligarh, 1954.
Faruqi, Nisar Ahmad, *Deed-o-Daryaft*, Delhi, 1964.
Faruqi, Nisar Ahmad, *Talaash-i-Mir*, Delhi, 1974.
Haq, Maulvi Abdul, *Urdu Ki Ibtadai Nashw-o-Numa Men Sufiya-i-Karam Ka Kam*, Aligarh, 1968.
Haq, Sanaul, *Mir Aur Sauda Ka Daur*, Karachi, 1965.
Hasan, Muhammad, *Delhi Men Urdu Shairi Ka Tahzibi aur Fikri Pas Manzar, 1707-1815*, 2nd Edition, Delhi, 1983.
Hasan, Muhammad, *Mutala-i-Sauda*, Lucknow, 1965.
Hashmi, Nurul Hasan, *Dilli Ka Dabistan-i-Shairi*, Lucknow, 1971.
Hashmi, Nasiruddin, *Dakhin Men Urdu*, Lucknow, 1963.
Islam, Khurshidul, *Tanqidin*, Aligarh, 1964.
Jafar, Salim, (ed.), *Gulzar-i-Nazir*, Allahabad, 1951.
Jain, Gian Chand, *Urdu Masnavi Shimali Hind Men*, Aligarh, 1969.
Jalibi, Jamil, *Muhammad Taqi Mir*, Delhi, 1983.
Makhmoor Akbarabadi, *Roohi Nazir*, Lucknow, 1978.
Muhammad, Syed, (ed.), *Masnaviyat-i-Mir*, Haiderabad, 1945.
Nizami, K.A., *Tarikh-i-Mashaikh-i-Chisht*, Vol. V, Delhi, 1984.
Qureshi, Abdur Razzaq, *Mirza Mazhar Jan-i-janan aur Unka Kalam*, Bombay, 1961.
Raza, Jafar, *Mir Ki Chand Masnaviyan*, Allahabad, 1968.
Sahr, Abu Muhammad, *Urdu Men Qasida Nigari*, Lucknow, 1979.
Sajjad, Syed, *Ab-i-Hayat Ka Tanqidi Aur Tahqiqi Mutala*, Delhi, 1978.
Sarwani, Abdul, Qadir, *Urdu Ki Adabi Tarikh*, Haiderabad, 1958.
Sarwani, Abdul Qadir, *Siraj-i-Sakhun*, Haiderabad, 1936.
Shabaz, Abdul Ghafoor, *Zindagani-i-Benazir*, Muhammed Husain (ed.), New Delhi, 1981.
Shirani, Mahmud, *Punjab Men Urdu*, Lahore, 1949.

Siddiqi, Aqiq Ahmad, *Qasaid-i-Sauda*, Aligarh, 1976.
Srivastava, G.S., *Urdu Shairi Ki Irtqa Men Hindu Shuara ka Hissa*, Allahabad, 1969.
Umar, Muhammad, *Atharven Sadi Men Hindustani Muashrat*, New Delhi, 1973.
Zor, Mohiuddin Qadiri, *Sarguzasht Hatim*, Haiderabad, 1944.
Zulfiqar, Ghulam Husain, *Shah Hatim, Halaat Aur Kalam*, Lahore, 1964.

English

Ahmad, Aziz, *Studies in Islamic Culture in the Indian Environment*, Oxford, 1964.
Ahmad, Aziz, *An Intellectual History of Islam in India*, Edinburgh, 1969.
Ahmad, Imtiaz, (ed.), *Ritual and Religion Among Muslims in India*, Delhi, 1981.
Alam, Muzaffar, *The Crisis of Empire in Mughal North India, Awadh and Punjab, 1707-48*, New Delhi, 1986.
Arberry, A.J., *Sufism: An Account of the Mystics of Islam*, London, 1950.
Bailey, T.G., *A History of Urdu Literature*, New Delhi, 1979.
Banga, Indu, *Agrarian System of the Sikhs. Late 18th and early 19th century*, New Delhi, 1978.
Barnett, R., *North India Between Empires, Awadh, the Mughals and the British*, Berkeley, 1980.
Bayly, C.A., *Rulers, Townsmen and Bazaars*, Cambridge, 1983.
Beal, T.W., *Oriental Biographical Dictionary*, (ed.) H.C. Keene, London, 1947.
Bearce, George, *British Attitudes Towards India, 1784-1858*, London, 1961.
Chandra, Satish, *Parties and Politics at the Mughal Court*, 2nd edition, New Delhi, 1972.
Chandra, Satish, *Medieval India, Society, Jagirdari Crisis and the Village*, New Delhi, 1982.
Chandra, Satish, *The Eighteenth Century in India: Its Economy and the Role of the Marathas, the Jats, the Sikhs and the Afghans*, Calcutta, 1986.
Chicherov, A.I., *India Economic Development in the* 16th to 18th *Centuries*, Moscow, 1971.
Datta, K.K., *Shah Alam II and the East India Company*, Calcutta, 1965.
Datta, K.K., *Survey of India's social and economic condition in the eighteenth century*, Calcutta, 1961.

Dharma Kumar, (ed.), *The Cambridge Economic History of India*, Volume II, New Delhi, 1984.

Eaton, Richard Maxwell, *Sufis of Bijapur, 1300-1700, Social Roles of Sufis in Medieval India*, New Jersey, 1978.

Elliot, Sir, H.M. and John Downson, *The History of India as told by its own historians*, Volumes VII, VIII, Allahabad, 1964.

Franklin, W., *The History of the Reign of Shah Aulum*, Reprint, Lucknow, 1974.

Friedmann, Y., *Shaikh Ahmad Sirhindi*, Montreal, 1971.

Frykenberg, R.E., *Land control and social structure in Indian history*, Wisconsin, 1969.

Frykenberg, R.E., (ed.), *Delhi Through The Ages*, New Delhi, 1986.

Goetz, H., *Crisis of the Indian civilization in the eighteenth and early nineteenth centuries*, Calcutta, 1938.

Goswamy, B.N. and G.S. Grewal, *The Mughal and the Sikh Rulers and Vaishnavas of Pindori*, Simla, 1969.

Habib, Irfan, *Agrarian System of Mughal India*, Bombay, 1963.

Hasan, Mohammad, *Nazir Akbarabadi*, New Delhi, 1973.

Hasan, Nurul, *Thoughts, on Agrarian Relations in Mughal India*, New Delhi, 1973.

Heestermann, J.C. (ed.), *The Inner Conflict of Tradition*, Chicago, 1985.

Irvine, W., *Later Mughals*, 2 Volumes, Calcutta, 1922.

Kabir, Hamayun, *Britain and India*, Calcutta, 1960.

Karim, Abdul, *Murshid Quli Khan and His Times*, Dacca, 1963.

Khan, Yusuf Husain, *Glimpses of Medieval Indian Culture*, Bombay, 1957.

Khan, Yusuf Husain, *Nizamulmulk Asaf Jah I: The Founder of Haiderabad State*, Manglore, 1936.

Leonard, K., *The Kayasthas of Haiderabad: The Social History of an Indian Caste*, Berkeley, 1978.

Lockhart, L., *Nadir Shah*, Lahore, 1976.

Malik, Zahiruddin; *The Reign of Muhammad Shah*, Bombay, 1977.

Medieval India, *A Miscellany*, Volume IV, Bombay, 1977.

Moreland, W.H., *From Akbar to Aurangzeb*, New Delhi, 1972.

Mujeeb, Muhammad, *The Indian Muslims*, London, 1969.

Naqvi, H.K., *Urban centres and industries in upper India 1556-1803*, London, 1968.

Pavlov, V.I., *Indian Capitalist Class: A Historical Perspective*, Delhi, 1964.

Qureshi, I.H., *The Muslim Community of the Indo-Pakistan Subcontinent*, The Hague, 1962.

Raghuvanshi, V.P.S., *Indian Society in the eighteenth century*, New Delhi, 1969.

Richards, D.S., *Islam and Trade of Asia*, Pennsylvania, 1970.

Rizvi, S.A.A., *Shahwaliullah and His Times*, Canberra, 1980.

Rizvi, S.A.A., *A History of Sufism in India*, Volume II, New Delhi, 1983.

Rizvi, S.A.A., *Shah Abdul Aziz, Puritanism, Sectarian Polemics and Jihad*, Canberra, 1982.

Roy, Asim, *The Islamic Syncretistic Tradition in Bengal*, New Jersey, 1983.

Russell, Ralph and Khurshidul Islam, *Three Mughal Poets*, London, 1969.

Sadiq, Muhammad, *A History of Urdu Literature*, New Delhi, 1984.

Sarkar, J.N., *Fall of the Mughal Empire*, 4 Volumes, New Delhi, 1971.

Sarkar, J.N., *Nadir Shah in India*, reprint, Calcutta, 1973.

Saxena, R.B., *History of Urdu Literature*, Allahabad, 1927.

Schacht, J. and C.E. Bosworth, (ed.), *The Legacy of Islam*, Oxford, 1974.

Schimmel, Annmarie, *Mystical dimensions of Islam*, N. Carolina, 1975.

Schimmel, A., *Classical Urdu literature from the beginning to Iqbal*, Wiesbaden, 1975.

Schimmel, A., *Sindhi Literature*, Wiesbaden, 1974.

Schimmel, A., *Islam in the Indian subcontinent*, Leiden, 1980.

Schimmel, A., *Pain and Grace: A study of two mystical writers of the eighteenth century Muslim India*, Lieden, 1976.

Shobha, Savitri Chandra, *Social life and Concepts in the Medieval Hindi Bakhti Poetry*, New Delhi, 1983.

Sen, Sukumar, *A History of Bengali Literature*, New Delhi, 1960.

Siddiqi, N.A., *Land Revenue Administration under the Mughals, 1700-1750*, Bombay, 1970.

Sinha, M., *History of Oriya Literature*, New Delhi, 1962.

Sinha, N.K., *Economic History of Bengal*, Calcutta, 1962.

Spear, P., *Twilight of the Mughals*, New Delhi, 1969.

Srivastava, A.L., *Shujauddaulah of Awadh*, Agra, 1974.

Tarachand, *Influence of Islam on Indian Culture*, Allahabad, 1963.

Tarachand, *Society and State in the Mughal period*, Delhi, 1961.

Trimingham, J.S., *The Sufi orders in Islam*, Oxford, 1971.

Zaehner, R.C., *Hindu Muslim Mysticism*, London, 1960.

Published Articles

Ahmad, Imtiaz, 'The Ashraf Ajlaf dichotomy in Muslim Social Structure', *Economic and Social History Review*, 1966.

Ajkal, April, 1984.

Ali, Athar, 'Towards a Reinterpretation of the Mughal Empire', *Journal of Royal Asiatic Society*, 1978.

Bearce, George, 'Intellectual and cultural characteristics of India in a changing era 1740-1800', *Journal of Asian Studies*, November, 1965.

Calkins, P., 'The formation of a regionally oriented ruling group in Bengal', Journal of Asian Studies, XXX, 1971.

Delhi College Magazine, *Mir Number*, 1962.

Faruqi, Ziaul Hasan, 'Orthodoxy and Heterodoxy in Indian Islam'. *Islam and the Modern Age*, 1979.

Friedmann, Y., 'Medieval Muslim view of Indian religion', *Journal of American and Oriental Society*, 1975.

Habib, Irfan, 'Potentialities of Capitalistic Development', *Journal of Economic History*, 1969.

Hasan, Nural, 'Presidential Address', *Proceedings of Indian History Congress*, 1961.

Irvine, W., 'Ahmad Shah Abdali and the Indian Wazir, Imadulmulk', *Indian Antiquary*, XXVI, 1907.

Lawrence, Bruce B., 'Islam in India', *Contributions to Asian Studies*, Volume, XVII, 1982.

Leonard, K., 'The Hyderabad Political System and its Participants', *Journal of Asian Studies*, XXX, 1971.

Malik, Zahiruddin, 'Some aspects of Mughal culture during the first half of the eighteenth century', *Studies in Islam*, Volume II, 1965.

Schimmel, A., 'Reflections of Popular Muslim Poetry', *Contributions to Asian Studies*, Volume XVIII, Leiden, 1982.

Singh, Dilbagh, 'The Role of Mahajan in the Rural Economy in Eastern Rajasthan, *Social Scientist*, 1974.

INDEX